SPEED
TO SPARE

SPEED
TO SPARE

BEYER SPEED FIGURES UNCOVERED

by

Joe Cardello

DRF Press
NEW YORK

All past performances for races after July 22, 1998,
provided by Equibase Company.

Published by
Daily Racing Form Press
100 Broadway, 7th Floor
New York, NY 10005

ISBN: 0-9700147-6-7
Library of Congress Control Number: 2002114412

Cover and jacket designed by Chris Donofry

Text design by Neuwirth and Associates

Printed in the United States of America

Contents

Acknowledgments   vii

Introduction   xi

CHAPTER 1: Beyer Basics   1

CHAPTER 2: Top Beyers   9

CHAPTER 3: Beyer Bouncers   27

CHAPTER 4: Beyer Patterns and Cycles   47

CHAPTER 5: Beyers on Grass   67

CHAPTER 6: Thinking Beyer   75

CHAPTER 7: Conclusion: Beyer Limits   103

Acknowledgments

IN MORE THAN 30 years of horseplaying I've been very fortunate in my friends. In 20 years at the New York tracks I enjoyed the company of a wide variety of interesting players: Jack Brown, Joe DeFillipo, Gary DeVincenzi, Sandy Hirsch, Mark Hopkins, Paul Mellos, Connie Merjos, Harvey Pack, Jan Person, Dick Sypher, and Richie Crost, aka "The Beard"—just to mention a few. Each one had at least a piece of the puzzle.

In 12 years on the Maryland circuit I found equally strong and stimulating friends: Bob Beck, Don Flecksteiner, Mike Geralis, Austin Mittler, Dave Rodman, and Peter Sherman. I happily endured the caustic comments and encyclopedic knowledge of gaming-industry economist, equine investor, and longtime pal Maury Wolff. And I benefited enormously from the advice and companionship of a wise and good friend, Pete Silberman.

Good fortune followed me to Hialeah, where I basked in the matchless company of Pete Axthelm, and to the Las Vegas race books, where I have been blessed with another great friend, Joe

Kraus, whose racing library got me off to a fast start in the writing of this book.

But I must make more particular and most grateful mention of two longtime friends and horseplaying pros—Andy Beyer and Paul Cornman—who have helped me in countless ways over many years and in many places. They have always been terrific friends, as well as valuable allies in the parimutuel struggle.

My special thanks also to Steven Crist and Dean Keppler of *Daily Racing Form* for letting me take a shot at this book. And to Robin Foster for a superb job of editing, and for taking all the pain out of the process. And, once again, to Andy Beyer for trusting me with this task, and for introducing me to the wonderful world of the figs.

To MJ

INTRODUCTION
by Andrew Beyer

SPEED HANDICAPPERS FREQUENTLY express nostalgia for the good old days, before most bettors appreciated the importance of horses' final times, before many books and articles had been written on the subject, and before the Beyer Speed Figures were included in *Daily Racing Form* past performances. In the 1970's and earlier, a horseplayer who used figures had a formidable edge over his parimutuel rivals. He could obtain huge odds on a horse whose record was superficially poor but whose figures revealed that he was the fastest member of a field. If a handicapper had good speed figures, he didn't need much else to succeed. I would guess that simply playing the horse with the top speed figure in every race would have shown a flat-bet profit over a long period of time.

Those days are gone, of course. As most of the American racing community—owners, trainers, and breeders, as well as bettors—has recognized the supreme importance of speed figures, the odds on standout horses have dropped. Betting blindly on top-figure horses is no longer an easy source of profits. When I wrote

Beyer on Speed in 1993, *Daily Racing Form* analyzed 10,000 races and found that horses with an edge of three or more points over their opposition won 29 percent of the time, but betting them all produced a 7.5 percent loss.

Even so, opportunities from figures certainly haven't disappeared, as the 2002 Kentucky Derby proved. War Emblem came to Churchill Downs after running a Beyer Speed Figure of 112 in his last start, the Illinois Derby—the best number recorded by any member of his Thoroughbred generation. None of his Derby rivals had earned better than a 104 in his most recent start. In a run-of-the-mill race, a horse with such a towering advantage would have been solidly bet, and perhaps overbet. But the wagering public (myself included) had a blind spot about War Emblem, and when he led all the way, virtually duplicating his Illinois performance, he paid $43 to win. To profit from figures today, a horseplayer may have to look harder for the right spots, and to use figures with some ingenuity, but money-making opportunities are still abundant.

How to find them is the theme of this book, and Joe Cardello is uniquely qualified to write it. Joe and I have been friends since the 1970's, when we met at the New York tracks and discovered a common bond: Each of us had been on an academic path until we realized that horse racing was the greatest intellectual challenge of them all. Joe had been working on a doctoral dissertation in history at SUNY at Stoneybrook; when a budget cut eliminated his fellowship, he was forced to earn money at the track. He started betting harness races before shifting to Thoroughbreds, and he brought with him the typical harness bettor's keen sense of the importance of horses' trips. While I was slavishly devoted to my speed figures and thought there was no other way to play the game, Joe was one of the first horseplayers I ever met who called himself a trip handicapper.

In 1991, when the short-lived *The Racing Times* planned to incorporate Beyer Speed Figures into its past performances, my partner Mark Hopkins and I needed more manpower to calculate the numbers, and I immediately thought of Joe. We indoctrinated him into our method, and he joined the fig-making team. In recent years he has written a column for *Daily Racing Form* about speed figures. As a handicapper, he relied on both figures and trips, but in recent years he has found his best betting situations by analyzing patterns in horses' figures.

I confess I have always been dubious about this approach to the game, which was popularized by adherents of the Thoro-Graph and Ragozin speed-figure "Sheets." Ragozin coined the term *bounce,* which has become part of the racetrack lexicon to describe a poor performance that follows a horse's peak effort. When the Sheet handicappers look for certain patterns in horses' numbers, they often do so myopically; they seem to think that patterns of figures are foreordained instead of being influenced by trips, track biases, pace, and countless other factors. On a given day a horse might run a figure of 60 or 80, depending on the way a race develops, and it is absurd to look at figures out of the context of the way they were earned.

Because his trip-handicapping background made him appreciate the game's subtleties, Joe brings a much less doctrinaire approach to the subject of figure patterns. He knows that horses aren't just numbers on a page. He knows, too, a handicapper must take into account the trainer as he analyzes a horse's changing performances. A horse might have run the figure of his life in his last start, portending a bounce, but if he did so after being claimed by a top trainer like Scott Lake, the bounce theory might have to be thrown out the window. But amid all the factors that confuse form cycles, Joe sees a large picture: Horses reach a peak, regress, and then cycle back to their top level. As he explains his theories, he will give readers of this book many fresh ideas about how to profit from Beyer Speed Figures.

SPEED
TO SPARE

BEYER BASICS

*T*HE BEYER SPEED FIGURES are right there in bold type—every day in your *Daily Racing Form*. But few handicappers really know the best ways to use them.

This book will offer some fresh ideas on the Beyer figures, their uses, and abuses. It is real-world stuff, providing practical insights and common, everyday examples. It is designed to help you integrate the Beyers into your overall handicapping and analyze them more effectively and more profitably. It contains no simple formulas, no magical numbers to add up, no rigid rules to follow. Handicapping is seldom if ever that simple. Learning to think intelligently and creatively with the Beyers—that's the key. And that's the goal of this book.

This book is *not* about how to calculate the Beyer Speed Figures. The methodology behind the Beyers has long been a matter of public record, most particularly in the books written by Andrew Beyer himself. And he is much better qualified to explain the philosophy and mechanics of his figures than I am. But I do encourage you to investigate how the figures are calculated, because, whatever speed figures you might be using, you should know how they are created. If you don't know how your figures are developed, or what exactly goes into them, you won't be able to use them properly—or decide whether it's worth using them at all.

Why do we need speed figures? Why can't we just use the final time of a race to tell us how fast a horse ran?

There are two basic reasons why final times are inadequate and, indeed, can be completely misleading. First, races are run at many different distances, and it doesn't help us much to say that one horse ran a mile in 1:36 while his rival ran $1^{1}/_{8}$ miles in 1:48.40. In order to compare times at so many different distances, we need to translate those times into a number. This we do by analyzing a mountain of data to establish the relationships of times at all American tracks, so that we know, for example, that at Santa Anita running one mile in 1:35 is a performance equal to running $1^{1}/_{8}$ miles in 1:48.

Second, the inherent speed of racing surfaces can vary greatly from track to track, from day to day, even from race to race. A horse that runs nine furlongs in 1:48 over a glib Santa Anita track might deliver the same effort at Fair Grounds and go in 1:50. Actual running times need to be adjusted to reflect these differences. If the dirt track at Belmont Park, for example, is three inches deep on Wednesday and four inches deep on Thursday, the final times of the races run on those two days have to be adjusted accordingly. This requires the calculation of a "track variant," which is added to or subtracted from the final time of a race.

The methods behind the creation of a track variant were explained in great detail by Andrew Beyer in his first book, *Picking Winners,* as well as in his more recent *Beyer on Speed.* Without repeating all the complexities analyzed in Beyer's works, suffice it to say that, in order to produce a track variant, we estimate how fast each race on a card ought to be run and compare that estimate with the actual final time. For example, if a horse wins a $1^1/_8$-mile race in 1:48, which has a speed rating of 122 in our system, and does it on a very fast track with a variant of minus 20, that horse earns a figure of 102.

So, basically, speed figures take the time of a race and translate it into something useful for the handicapper, something he can use to compare the relative speeds and abilities of horses that have run at different distances, at different racetracks, and on different days at the same racetrack. These numbers are applicable across the board, at all North American racetracks. So an 82 run at one mile represents the same quality of speed and ability as an 82 at six furlongs, and an 82 run at Calder Race Course equals an 82 run at Hollywood Park or anywhere else. As Andrew Beyer describes it, "The Beyer figures provide a universal language with which to talk about horses' ability."

It should be remembered, of course, that the Beyer figures measure how fast a horse ran in *past* races. That might seem self-evident, but it should always be kept in mind. Speed figures are part of the *past*-performance lines. They're part of that horse's history. They are not automatic predictors or guarantors of how that horse will perform on any given day in the future. That's where the art of handicapping comes in.

There are important differences among the many speed-figure products now available to the betting public, and you need to know what they are. Many of these products are sold as separate entities, fully detached from all the other vital elements of a horse's record. Others attempt to assign a numerical value to factors such as wind, weight, and even ground loss. They all have their claims and they all have their value.

As for the nature of the Beyer Speed Figures, they are what might be termed "pure" speed figures. They are based on final time, and final time *only*, adjusted for different track conditions on different days and at different racetracks. As a measure of time only, they can only be fully appreciated in the context of other handicapping variables. For that reason, their place as only one element in the past-performance lines published by *Daily Racing Form* is highly symbolic.

Speed figures are just one variable—some might say the most vital and indispensable variable—among many other significant factors: pace, distance, surface, trips, class, trainer, jockey, track conditions, biases, odds, equipment, layoffs, and on and on. But, despite all these familiar complexities and interrelationships, a Thoroughbred horse race is still most fundamentally a function of speed and time. What you are looking for is the horse or horses ready to run the fastest in any particular field, and under today's particular conditions. So it would not be too much to call speed figures the leading factor in handicapping—the starting point in evaluating any race. In *Daily Racing Form* past-performance lines, the Beyer Speed Figures should be considered primus inter pares—the first among equals.

At the most basic level, speed figures should be used to break down a race according to the most tested handicapping wisdom:

1. **First, eliminate the losers.** That's probably the earliest lesson any of us learned about handicapping. And the Beyer figures are the quickest, most reliable way to weed out the false pretenders and isolate the main contenders. It doesn't take long to see which horses just aren't fast enough to compete. When a horse's speed figures are consistently and substantially behind his competitors'—with little prospect of dramatic improvement—that horse can be safely eliminated. Once in a long while such a horse will jump up without warning and upset all your careful logic and analysis. These things happen in horse racing. You simply have to turn the page to the next race—and, in this age of multisignal simulcasting, you won't have too long to wait. That next race will be along in a matter of seconds.

2. **Identify closely matched fields.** When a large number of horses in any particular field have Beyers that cluster around a certain two or three numbers, that's usually a sign that you should move on to the next race, that the race is just too competitive. Unless you can come up with some special insight that will separate these close contenders, the better part of wisdom is to pass. But, as we will see, in these contentious situations, the Beyer Speed Figures can give you that special angle that could separate a horse from the rest of the pack. Then you could quickly turn a seemingly inscrutable race into a big-value play. The following pages will offer a variety of ways to help you in making these critical distinctions. They will help you judge which horses can be expected to continue to perform at the same level, which horses might decline, and which horses can be projected to improve. Such a dynamic approach is essential if you want to get value for your money.

3. **Put reputations to the test.** The Beyer figures give you an effective, reliable reality check. When you see a runaway winner, or you're impressed by a horse running well despite a tough trip, hold back on any final judgments until the returns are in from the Beyer figures. If the figure is disappointing, you might have to temper your enthusiasm for that horse next time he runs. If the figure is extremely high, you might have to wonder whether the extraordinary effort might actually have taken too much out of the horse. Speed figures provide that all-important reality check. They add an objective measure to your visual impressions. They can keep you off unprofitable bandwagons, and they can help you to distinguish between real ability and mere reputation.

After the Beyers have helped you with these fundamental tasks, that's when the real fun begins. That's when you get into the more detailed analysis that will be the main focus of this book. In that concentrated effort lies the excitement and stimulation of one of the world's most challenging activities: Thoroughbred handicapping.

Of course, writing about handicapping is relatively easy. After all, everything looks more logical on paper, and race results (at least most race results) are easily explainable after the fact. Actual real-life handicapping, as we all know, is much harder. And betting and winning is more difficult still. So the point of a handicapping book should not be simply to add to our accumulated knowledge about horseplaying. The point should be to add to our *useful* knowledge. You don't need more masses of data and mind-boggling, contradictory percentage angles to clutter your thinking. While the following pages will present the occasional statistical study, these will always be presented merely as guidelines. They will *not* be accompanied by any sort of dogma or instructions. They will be offered with that healthy dose of skepticism that should accompany all statistics and percentages in the handicapper's world.

Today's horseplayer doesn't need another volume that looks more like a mathematics text than a handicapping book. And he doesn't need any more books that appear to come from some antiseptic research lab, divorced from the disorderly, often chaotic stress and strain of the parimutuel struggle. Instead, what most horseplayers would appreciate is some greater insight into real-life handicapping situations, into the wide variety of circumstances that all players inevitably face every racing day. This book will try to describe as many of these typical situations as it can, but there's just no way to cover every type of handicapping problem. All races are different. Every puzzle is unique. So the important challenge is to provide analysis and examples that will help to demonstrate the basic thought processes involved in using the Beyer Speed Figures—ways of thinking that will, it is hoped, serve the player well in many different situations.

That's what this book is all about, so let's get to it.

A Note on Examples

If you look long enough and go back far enough, you can find examples to "prove" almost any handicapping theory. That's why the examples in this book (with very few exceptions) are taken from a limited three-month period from late summer to early fall 2002. Every effort has been made to avoid dredging up examples from the long and distant past. Instead, the examples in the following pages have been chosen primarily from the common, ordinary races that most of us have to deal with on a day-to-day basis. And they have been selected from a more concentrated period in order to demonstrate just how effective the Beyer figures can be in *real* time at the races—providing a substantial number of high-value plays, in a relatively short span of time, at a limited number of racetracks. It is my hope that this approach will offer the reader a more realistic, more helpful guide to real-life Thoroughbred handicapping.

TOP BEYERS

*T*HE BEYER SPEED FIGURE is a number, but it's not a statistic. When you study 1,000 races and you discover that approximately 28 percent to 30 percent of top Beyer figures win those races, then you have a statistic. And in recent years we've seen a tremendous proliferation of such statistics—a virtual plague of computer-generated percentages. Sire X wins with 11 percent of his first-time starters. Sire Y wins 13 percent with first-timers on the turf. Trainer A wins 18 percent of the time immediately after a claim. Trainer B wins 16 percent of the time when stretching a horse out the second start after a layoff. And on and on and on. How useful are all these to the average horseplayer?

Racing statistics generally reside in the 6 percent to 19 percent range. The few trainers or jockeys who win more than 20 percent of the time stand out high above the rest. Those who win less than 5 percent will have a tough time surviving. My advice would be to ignore all statistics that inhabit that overpopulated 6 percent to 19 percent range. Only if a horse, or sire, or trainer, or handicapping angle wins 5 percent or less, or 20 percent or more—only then would I consider factoring it into my handicapping. For practical horseplaying purposes there is no significant difference between a trainer or sire or anything else that wins 12 percent and another that wins 17 percent. Stick with the useful extremes—they might be suggestive of something valuable.

I've written a lot about baseball history, so I know that statistics can be fascinating. But if you're going to use them as a basis for wagering your hard-earned money, then you need them to be more than just entertainment or of purely academic interest. You want to have confidence in their ability to say something predictive about the future. And, unfortunately, most of the statistics we see in racing cannot hope to predict much of anything on a race-to-race basis—especially anything of parimutuel value. Statistical extrapolations are abstractions, and you don't want to be betting on too many abstractions.

Having said all that, there are certain broader percentages that do serve an important function. They don't produce specific winners, and they can't help you much in handicapping any particular race. But they do provide a general context for understanding the game. For example, there's the oldest and best known statistic of all: that favorites win one out of every three races. In-depth studies of favorites have never been able to tell us which favorites we're supposed to bet and which favorites we're supposed to avoid. In other words, they can't help us to decide how any particular favorite will run in today's fifth at Philly Park. Instead, their value is more general in telling us that favorites need to be given special attention because, on average, they win three times every racing day. You can't make money just betting favorites, but, because they win at such a high and reliable rate, you often start analyzing a race by evaluating the strengths and weaknesses of the favorite. And, by definition, you can get value if you can beat them.

When the Beyer Speed Figures first began to appear regularly in print in *The Racing Times* in 1991, a small cadre of men with big, powerful computers went to work on them, just as an earlier generation (minus the computers, of course) had done with betting favorites. Two of these studies stand out for their comprehensiveness and scope:

▶ In 1993 SportsStat studied 11,394 sprint races. The top Beyer figure won 28.58 percent of the races. In route races the percentage was 25.41 percent.
▶ In 1996 Jim Bayle of SportsStat studied 16,450 races. The top Beyer figure won 25.4 percent.

In my own studies I found somewhat similar but slightly higher results, even at some of the lower-echelon racetracks:

▶ At the Beulah Park winter/spring meeting in 2002, the top figure won 28.9 percent.
▶ At Northlands Park (in Edmonton) in 2001, the top figure won 26 percent.
▶ At River Downs in 2002, the top figure won 31.2 percent.

(If you don't include co-top figures, the percentages decline slightly to 27 percent, 25 percent, and 29.4 percent, respectively.)

The percentage of winning top Beyer figures thus has many of the same characteristics as the venerable winning-favorites percentage. It is substantial (varying between 26 percent and 30 percent). It is consistent from year to year. And it applies to all types of tracks and under all sorts of conditions. As a result, it has become one of racing's few reliable constants.

Just as happened with favorites, the substantial percentage of winning top-Beyer figures has led to many studies that attempt to break the numbers down further, searching for some sort of profitable formula. These eager analysts turned the Beyers this way and that, and tested lots of propositions, trying to see whether you could make money just by following some corollary or subset of the Beyer Speed Figures. One study by Steven Davidowitz in *Betting Thoroughbreds* (second revised edition) concluded that "whenever comparisons are restricted between the top speed figures earned under the same conditions as today's race (same track conditions and distance, give or take $^{1}/_{16}$ miles) the horse with the top figure by at least two full points in sprints and three points in routes wins about 35% of all starts at a slight flat-bet profit." One of the SportsStat studies distinguished between top-figure horses with only a one-point edge over their competition (they won only 21.3 percent) and those with as much as an eight-point differential (they won 31 percent). Of course, in the latter case, the payoffs quite logically declined.

This raises a very practical question of definition. For the purposes of general statistical study, the top Beyer in any race is defined as the horse with the highest figure in its previous race on that surface (dirt or turf), regardless of distance, track conditions, trips, post positions, or any other variable. But in the real world of handicapping, that definition has precious little value. Figure-making is, after all, as much art as science. It is a very human activity—an attempt by some very human person to make numerical sense out of a very complicated, often intractable set of racing conditions and race results. Every speed figure is produced by an individual struggling with sometimes inadequate, often bewildering, and occasionally even contradictory data from any particular racing day.

So, although the art has become more and more refined and sophisticated over the years, it is still not a perfect science—and it never will be. Every speed figure represents the most accurate number that experienced, conscientious experts can calculate based on the available evidence. It cannot be considered in the same category with some extremely precise, unalterable scientific fact tested under carefully controlled laboratory conditions. Racing cannot hope to aspire to such certainty or precision. That's just not the nature of the beast.

The point here is that, given the margin of error (as small as humanly possible, we hope) implicit in the vagaries of figure-making, a single-point difference in Beyer figures, or even two points in sprints, is virtually meaningless in the real world of racing. If you have one horse that ran a top Beyer of 82 at six furlongs, and another horse that just ran an 81, or even an 80, for all practical purposes they are indistinguishable. There is no meaningful sense in which that 82 can be considered a "top" figure. Minuscule edges in statistics of *any* kind have no practical meaning in Thoroughbred racing. As a number of these studies have demonstrated (including those by Davidowitz, Beyer, and SportsStat), the practical value of a top figure only becomes meaningful when that horse has at least a three-point edge in sprints over the next-best figure, and at least two points in routes.

In *Daily Racing Form*'s study of top Beyers with at least a three-point edge (published in *Beyer on Speed*), that more clear-cut top-figure horse won 29 percent of the time. Unfortunately, but not surprisingly, that 29 percent rate still didn't turn a flat-bet profit. Just as with favorites, you can't make money automatically betting the top Beyer figure, although you can come amazingly close. But, again, just as with favorites, the top-figure horse in any race is often the starting point for handicappers using the Beyer Speed Figures.

When they start analyzing a particular race, some experienced players begin by identifying the top Beyer and then trying to see if that horse can be expected to repeat that effort. In other words, they try to determine, after careful analysis, whether that horse can be confidently supported at the windows—whether, under today's specific conditions, he will justify his top-figure status. My personal approach is somewhat different. I want to identify the top Beyer so that I can use it as a target to bet against. There's a somewhat different emphasis here, but not necessarily any fundamental conflict. Both approaches recognize the importance of isolating and dissecting the top-figure horse (who is very often the betting favorite). Both approaches can ultimately lead to the same conclusion, for or against. And they both start with versions of the same question: How solid, or how vulnerable, is the top Beyer horse? This is quickly followed by the next obvious question: If he's solid, is the top figure worth betting at the price?

In the third race at Aqueduct on October 31, Rosie Is A Leader came as close to the ideal top-figure horse as you're likely to get.

Her recent figure of 74 was more than 10 points higher than any other horse in the field, and there were no troubling negatives in her form. There was no long layoff. There was no severe drop or drastic rise in class. There was no apparent danger of a "bounce," since she had actually run a 74 on July 6 and a 78 on August 22. She didn't appear to be hampered by any one-dimensional running style that could create problems for her if she encountered adverse circumstances. There were no obvious prospects of dramatic improvement from her competition, except perhaps for Clear Pouch, who had a 63 Beyer on August 8, and then had run 29-53-55, the latter two figures perhaps compromised by sloppy tracks. The distance of seven furlongs could have presented some problem for Rosie Is A Leader, but that didn't appear likely in this relatively weak field.

So, Rosie Is A Leader had the clear top figure and no serious negatives. All in all, a solid top Beyer, no doubt. There was only one problem: her price. Not surprisingly, Rosie was a 4-5 favorite. Not surprisingly, she won with little trouble, paying $3.90. Clear Pouch finished a strong second, with the exacta returning $15.80.

Of course, in this modern age of multiple and wide-ranging exotics, a horse like Rosie Is A Leader could have value well beyond her straight price. She was the type of top-figure horse you could confidently single in pick threes, or at the start of the pick six, so there was certainly some merit in recognizing her overwhelming credentials. But for many other players it's that short price that casts a shadow over a great number of these top-figure winners.

This theme was driven home shortly after Rosie won at Aqueduct. A few minutes later there was another apparently solid figure horse in Calder's fourth race. Actcess had put together six solid Beyers in a row: 68-65-56-61-63-59. In addition, there was a late scratch of the only other potential front-runner, so Actcess now looked like the lone speed as well as the top figure. (Technically, she was not actually the top figure. Another horse had run a 63 in her previous start, but that was so far above any of her previous efforts that she had the look of a likely bounce—a subject we will explore in depth in the next chapter.) No other horse came close to matching Actcess's consistently higher figures.

With these overwhelming recommendations, Actcess quite predictably went off at odds of 3-5. Unfortunately, when the gates opened she took her time walking out, had to rush up early, couldn't get to the lead, chased the pace on the outside, and then faded badly in the stretch. Actcess's fate provided a needed reminder of the obvious: Horses with overwhelming speed-figure edges nearly always go off at short prices. They have their limited uses, depending on what types of bets you're in the habit of making. But, since so many things can go wrong in any particular race—even for powerful-looking speed-figure types—the short-priced, obvious top-Beyer horse is generally best avoided.

Of course, the fact remains that the top-figure horse does win somewhere between 26 percent and 30 percent of the time. But that includes all kinds of horses, from the Secretariats and

Ruffians of the racing world all the way down to such distinctly lesser lights as Phickled Fate, Bailey's Baby, and Halve It All. In his only lifetime start, Phickled Fate had chased the pace on a sloppy track in a $25,000 maiden claimer. That effort earned him the top Beyer in his next start at Delaware against a field of $12,500 maidens. That best Beyer was a lofty 22. He won, but he was 6-5 in a field full of mysterious drop-downs, lightly raced horses, and hard-to-evaluate first-time starters. Phickled Fate won, but he could hardly be called a good bet. The same could be said of Bailey's Baby, who won Laurel's opener on October 23 with an inglorious top Beyer of 14. And he was 4-5. Finally, there was Halve It All, the winner of Charles Town's first race on September 13. He actually went to the post with the astounding top Beyer figure of 5!

Clearly, not all top Beyers are created equal, and not every top-Beyer winner is worth betting. As in all handicapping situations, selectivity is the key. But there are at least two general situations when you should aggressively exploit the superiority of a top Beyer figure.

1. When the public is distracted, as it sometimes is, by big-name trainers or jockeys, or by horses with inflated reputations, it can ignore a strong top-figure horse. If you can find no discernible flaws in the horse, and it fits in terms of class and distance, that's the time to take the value on a top Beyer. It's not a common occurrence, but you should be ready to exploit it when it does occur.

2. There are times when the game can be easy. Not very often, but sometimes. You just have to learn to recognize these transparent situations and take advantage of them. For example, in the first race at Delaware on August 21—a rather unappealing affair for cheap maiden claimers—there were only two possible contenders. Both horses had run Beyers in the 40's and had an improving figure pattern. No

one else had ever come close to the 40's in any recent race. One of these contenders, General Syd, went off at 2-5. I preferred him to Ibelieveitsours, his principal rival, although I couldn't see why one of these horses should be odds-on and the other one 6-1. A simple exacta box was in order. Ibelieveitsours won by two lengths. He ran a Beyer of 53. General Syd finished second, rounding out a $30.20 exacta.

One week later, at Delaware on August 28, the early daily double had a similar almost-too-easy look to it. In the first race, involving another forlorn group of low-level maidens going one mile, only one horse had Beyers in the 40's or could logically be expected to run Beyers at that level. That was Gold Kisses, whose 43 in her last race at one mile and 70 yards towered over this very weak bunch. She won easily by $3^{1}/_{2}$ lengths. The second race had a more crowded field of even cheaper maidens. Only two horses appeared to have any hope of running above 40 at the distance of $1^{1}/_{16}$ miles. Twice Around had earned a 42 Beyer in his last race when beaten soundly by much better horses, and Digamy had run a 44 while finishing second at today's level. Digamy won by one length, running another 44 Beyer. The daily double paid $9—what you can more typically expect for the terribly obvious.

When you have such a confluence of the obvious—when solid top Beyers find themselves in both ends of the daily double, or in one or more races in a pick three, pick four, or pick six—then you might be able to squeeze some value out of these logical short-priced winners.

Unfortunately, the great majority of races are a lot more complicated than these two examples at Delaware. Still, you should not fight against a clear top Beyer figure when the distance suits, the competition is weak, and there is nothing in the horse's figure pattern or the spacing of his races that might prevent him from running his race. Generally these will not be value plays. Most often they will be favorites, many of them very short-priced favorites. But, when the situation appears transparently clear and unambiguous, it might be worth exploiting. I wouldn't recommend it as a steady diet—in fact, such clear-and-easy situations don't arise often enough to satisfy your hunger. But when they do, you should be prepared for action. Such plays should certainly be among the weapons in your Beyer Speed Figure arsenal.

What types of top-figure horses should you be looking to play? There's just no way to establish any rules or guidelines on such a broad subject without getting into a review of every conceivable handicapping angle: distance, pace, trainer moves, track bias, post positions, class, and so on. But I would suggest the following: If you are looking to play a top-figure horse, look for something out of the ordinary, something a bit unusual, something that might deflect the public's attention just enough to create some value. If the top-figure horse ran a big race last time out—and it's right there up front in the most recent past-performance line—in 95 out of 100 cases that horse is going to be pounded at the windows. Of course, many of these horses run very well, but don't expect to get much value for your money. But if there's some edge, some oblique angle, some element of concealment to the top figure, then you might have something more worthwhile.

1. **The "hidden" figure.** Back in the ancient past, before the Beyer figures became common knowledge, a horse who earned a competitive figure when he was beaten many lengths in a very swiftly run race could slip by the public. If, for example, he was beaten $10^1/2$ lengths in a fast allowance heat but still had a 75 Beyer, he might be dropped down next time to a $35,000 claimer where that 75 topped the field. Fifteen years ago such a figure was well hidden behind the poor running line. Today, of course, you can't hide anything. Still, there are times when such horses will be decent value because of the doubt created in the public mind by the number of

beaten lengths in the horse's previous race. In Calder's first race on November 28, Pent Up Speed had run a 40 Beyer while finishing sixth, beaten 13 lengths. He was the top figure at 7-2. But Yukon Loot was the odds-on favorite because he had recently finished third with a figure of 38. Pent Up Speed defeated Yukon Loot by a half-length, paying $9.60.

2. **Cases of neglect.** In the sixth race at Calder on October 24, I could see why the public might want to make Suave Gentleman the favorite. But 3-5? That seemed a bit over the top. He was dropping from maiden special weight to maiden claiming $35,000, was adding Lasix and blinkers, and had wide trips in his two lifetime starts. But his unimpressive Beyers of 54 and 51 should have counseled some restraint. After all, a horse named Book of the Year had just run Beyers of 58 and 62. He was the clear top figure in the race and deserved a bit more respect than to be ignored at 7-2. During the running, Suave Gentleman tried to wire the field, became entangled in a speed duel, and tired in the very late stages. Book of the Year plodded along, ground it out late, and struggled to get up by a nose in the absolute last jump. He had a good setup and was not impressive at all, but, win or lose, he was good value.

3. **Back figure.** As I see it, a horse like Whenmyshipcomesin represents the most appealing kind of top-figure horse—a runner with at least an element of disguise or misdirection obscuring his latent talent.

8 Whenmyshipcomesin
Own:Carolina Stable
Red, White Chevron, Red Blocks On White
AGUILAR M (33 6 4 8 .18) 2002:(1046 160 .15)

B. c. 3 (Apr) KEESEP00 $24,000
Sire: Premiership (Exclusive Native) $5,000
Dam: Greenislandancer(Greinton*GB)
Br: Starsfell Farms Inc (Ky)
Tr: Estevez Manuel A(4 0 0 0 .00) 2002:(157 22 .14)

L 118

Life	9	1	3	1	$27,255	81	D.Fst	5	0	3	1	$11,190	70
2002	5	1	3	1	$25,440	81	Wet(335)	2	0	0	0	$1,450	50
2001	4	M	0	0	$1,815	71	Turf(260)	2	1	0	0	$14,615	81
Crc Ⓣ	2	1	0	0	$14,615	81	DstⓉ(310)	0	0	0	0	$0	–

17Oct02-5Crc	gd	1 Ⓣ	:231 :473 1:114 1:37	3↑ Md Sp Wt 24k	81	4	106½	97¼	73¾	54½	1¾	Aguilar M	L118b	3.80	83-17	Whnmyshpcomsn118¾ DrnkATost1181 Emolmnt1223	Slow start, up late	10
3Oct02-6Crc	fst	1	:252 :492 1:143 1:41	3↑ Md 25000 (25-22.5)	65	6	55	69	65½	56	35	Nunez E O	L118b	4.50	71-27	DMilo1174¼ TcticlBlus118¾ *Whnmyshipcomsin*1182¼	Slow start, up for 3rd	8
22Sep02-4Crc	fst	1	:251 :502 1:154 1:414	3↑ Md 25000 (25-22.5)	70	3	2hd	1½	1hd	2hd	22¼	Nunez E O	L118b	*1.00	70-31	**BlivICnFly**1182¼ Whnmyshpcomsn1181¼ TctclBlus1184¾	3 wide, outfinished	7
6Sep02-10Crc	fst	7f	:222 :452 1:113 1:253	3↑ Md 25000 (25-22.5)	66	5	2	77¼	68½	45	24¼	Nunez E O	L118b	2.40	82-12	ArtillryPunch1174¼ Whnmyshpcomsn118¾ VldFury1183½	4 wide, up for 2nd	8
10Aug02-3Crc	fst	7f	:223 :453 1:113 1:254	3↑ Md 22500 (25-22.5)	65	5	2	65¼	77	51¾	2hd	Nunez E O	L116b	16.70	85-15	SlyTrth118hd Whnmyshpcomsn116½ ***Mck'sMny***1182½	Steadied mid stretch	8
15Dec01-2Crc	fm	1 1/16 Ⓣ	:23 :472 1:11 1:43	Md Sp Wt 26k	71	4	109½	1113	913	69	64	Karamanos H A	L120b	31.70	77-19	**NiceBoy**1201¾ Minerveni120½ ConquringStorm120hd	Stdy early & 1st turn	12
26Nov01-6Crc	fst	7f	:23 :463 1:121 1:263	Md 32000 (32-30)	47	8	5	84¾	89¼	810	711½	Aguilar M	120b	7.00	70-19	IslndSkppr120hd Contrdcton1183½ SuprDprKd115no	Steadied start, outrun	9
5Nov01-10Crc	sly	1	:234 :484 1:154 1:443	Md 35000 (40-35)	42	2	55½	76¾	77½	78¼	47½	Aguilar M	116	3.30	60-28	CladdaughRing1181¼ *LateralPss*1183¾ SebstinLight1182½	Failed to menace	8
20Oct01-12Crc	sly	6f	:223 :47 1:001 1:134	Md 25000 (25-22.5)	50	1	10	97¼	87	75¾	44¾	Aguilar M	120f	14.30	70-16	GreatBaron1203¼ FightEm'all1201 StopToDnce118½	Poor start, willingly	10

WORKS: Oct31 **Crc 3f fst :37 B** *9/16* Sep3 **Crc 3f fst :384 B** *6/9* Aug3 **Crc 4f fst :51 B** *51/93*
TRAINER: Turf(30 .03 $0.32) Routes(143 .10 $1.02) Alw(62 .03 $0.22)

In the fifth race at Calder on October 17, Whenmyshipcomesin faced a full field of nine on the grass. Five of his competitors had earned figures in the low-to-mid 60's, and none of them looked to be on the verge of any significant improvement. Whenmyshipcomesin had already run a figure of 71, and that was as a 2-year-old, way back in December. With normal development he could be capable of running an even higher figure as a much more mature 3-year-old. You had to wonder why his trainer brought him back after a long layoff and ran him four times in maiden-claiming races on the dirt. Perhaps he didn't notice that his horse had jumped up from a mediocrity on the dirt to a competitive special-weight runner on the turf. Whatever the explanation, he finally put the horse back on the grass. The result was a big win, with Whenmyshipcomesin making a strong wide move and closing well in the middle of the course to draw away by nearly a length. He paid $9.60, running a big Beyer of 81. Others in the field showed surprising improvement, but Whenmyshipcomesin fulfilled the promise he had shown as a 2-year-old on the turf.

4. Top-fig plus. This is a rare deluxe top figure, a sort of higher-octane version of the best Beyer. Always Crown Royal is the perfect example.

In a lowly maiden claimer at Philadelphia on October 22, Always Crown Royal had the top Beyer figure from her last race. No other horse was within 12 points of that number. Except for the fact that she wasn't terribly talented, she looked solid in every way. She had good recent form. She had no gaps that might indicate any physical problems. She could handle today's distance of one mile and 70 yards, as proved by her strong (for today's field) performance at Monmouth on August 31. She was not dropping sharply in class. She showed no indication of any possible regression from a high Beyer since she had previously run a 46. So a 35 on the turn-back to six furlongs should certainly not have exhausted her in any way.

This last point holds the key to the "plus" in the top Beyer of Always Crown Royal. In her first four races she had improved from 24 to 39 to 46 (with one excusable break over a sloppy track). Now she was improving again, from 22 to 35 just before today's race. She was returning to her best distance, going around two turns, and showed every indication of being in good health and good form. A figure of 35 (the top figure in the race) would probably beat this field. But if she could improve again, as many horses do (a subject fully covered in a later chapter) to something in the 46 range, the rest of the field would be left wondering which way she went. After all, most of her nine competitors had never even earned a Beyer as high as 30. That's where the "plus" comes in: Her real figure edge on the field was potentially much greater than her recent 35 would indicate.

Always Crown Royal dominated this weak field. She dueled early, then chased the pace, dueled on the final turn, and drew off to an impressive win. And she had something else that added to her attractiveness. The public was betting a horse that had run big Beyers on the grass at a higher class level. But that horse's dirt races had been horrendous, with figures of 22 and 23. And now she was dropping all the way down to the lowest maiden claimer. Nevertheless, the public made her 2-1. Not only did that buoy the price on Always Crown Royal, but it also created greater value in the second and third slots for exactas and trifectas. Always

Crown Royal ended up paying $5.60. The exacta with a very logical horse (*not* the 2-1 shot) paid $34.60.

5. **Top fig (once removed).** Green Beret was not the horse he used to be, and he had been dropped down to a $10,000 claimer, which he won after a long layoff, earning a Beyer of 81. That would have made him the clear top figure on October 25 at Laurel in a $12,500 claimer. But Green Beret had put in a very poor effort in his last race on a sloppy track. If you were willing to put aside that effort because of the track condition—not always a wise idea—Green Beret had a big figure edge on the field. And he was a very generous 7-1. In addition, there were at least two big speed horses in the race, perhaps three—and Green Beret was a closer. You could certainly question Green Beret's physical condition, but if you thought he could come close to repeating that 81 you were rewarded in the very last jump with a $16 pay-off. His winning figure: another 81.

6. **The "de facto" top figure.** This angle applies primarily to young horses returning to the races after substantial layoffs. According to the numbers printed on the page, they do not have the top Beyer in the race. But if you take their top figure in the last few races before they were laid off, and then calculate for potential improvement over time, they could very well be the *actual* top figure. Take the example of Lady Adare:

The top figure in the November 20 race was Polish Silk with an 81. But Lady Adare had run a figure of 74 way back in early February when she was essentially still a 2-year-old. According to Andrew Beyer, for every month of a layoff we should add a point or a point and a half to a young horse's figure. That should give us the Beyer that a young horse could potentially run after a layoff. In Lady Adare's case, that would mean a possible improvement of between nine and 15 points. That would make her the top figure in this race. Of course, layoffs are treacherous things. As outsiders, handicappers cannot ever know for certain whether a horse is fit and ready, or still in one piece physically. In Lady Adare's case there were positive hints: She had a steady, long-lasting workout pattern, and she was not being dropped in class. Even so, such horses are always a risk. But at 9-1 odds, she was well worth it. She passed the ostensible top figure, Polish Silk, in the very late stages, creating an unusual exacta combining two top figures with very different claims to that exalted status. It paid $42.40.

The top Beyer figure—obvious, hidden, misdirected, de facto, or whatever—always has to be dealt with. You have to respect it in any race, at least up to a point. And, even if you can find fault with that horse, and you think he won't run as well this time out, you will often find yourself wondering whether you can bridge the gap between that top figure and any other contender.

Clearly, this frequent problem of closing the gap with the top figure is most difficult when the gap is the widest. The most dramatic recent example of this came in the 2002 Travers Stakes at Saratoga. Medaglia d' Oro had earned a phenomenal 120 Beyer in the Jim Dandy just three weeks earlier. He had taken that field wire to wire on a big speed-favoring day. Nobody thought he could duplicate that effort, so every self-respecting wise guy was sifting through the Travers field trying to find someone who could challenge the overwhelming favorite. Unfortunately, no one in the field had ever run a Beyer above 102—except Like A Hero, who had run back-to-back lifetime-best figures of 106-105 and seemed like a sure candidate to take a step backward. Repent looked the most interesting because he had run 102's back in February and April as he prepared for the Triple Crown. He was sidelined by an injury and was now returning after a $4\frac{1}{2}$-month layoff. As a more mature horse, and if he was extremely fit and sharp, he should be able to improve substantially on those 102's. But would that be enough to close the huge chasm that still remained between him and Medaglia d'Oro? Of course, it all depended on how much lower a Beyer the favorite would run in the Travers.

In the Travers, Medaglia d' Oro dropped seven points to a 113. Repent made a huge improvement of 10 points up to a 112. The top Beyer had looked vulnerable, but nobody could quite bridge the chasm.

The 2002 Hopeful Stakes at Saratoga provides the sort of closer call we more commonly have to deal with. Although it's always risky to make such statements when you're dealing with developing young 2-year-olds, the Hopeful looked like a two-horse affair—at least according to the Beyer figures. The question was, could Sky Mesa, with his impressive Beyer of 92 in winning his maiden, improve enough to close the gap with favorite Zavata, whose last two Beyers were 102 and 101? Sky Mesa's maiden victory had looked awesome. He showed every sign of being a very special horse. He also looked like he would get better going longer, and his connections had very publicly talked about him as more of a distance horse. He had every reason to improve in the stretch-out to seven furlongs in the Hopeful. In the other corner, Zavata had always looked like a sprinter, and his connections (including jockey Jerry Bailey) had talked about his possible distance limitations. Only nine points separated them, and for 2-year-olds this early in the season, that kind of gap would not be too difficult to bridge. If Zavata slipped at all, Sky Mesa's figure could easily overtake him. This was not the kind of huge gap faced by Medaglia d' Oro's opposition.

Sky Mesa powered by Zavata in the stretch to win by $1^{3}/_{4}$ lengths, improving his Beyer figure to 103. Zavata fell back to a 95, struggling to finish well back in third place.

Whether you are handicapping these elite races, or tackling your typical, everyday event, the top-Beyer horse should be squarely in your crosshairs. First, you should identify the top figure, just as you would identify the favorite (often the same horse). And second, you should see if you can beat him. This might sound strange—even perverse—coming from someone who produces Beyer Speed Figures for a living. But it's not in any way a criticism of the value or accuracy of the Beyer figures, or a lack of faith in their usefulness. It's simply a recognition of harsh parimutuel reality.

It's important to take an aggressive stand against many top figures, for two reasons:

1. First, just as with favorites, the great majority of races are won by a horse other than the top figure. In his study of 601 California winners in 1994, Mart Koivastik concluded: "The average winning Beyer figure was 10 points higher than its figure from the preceding race; the median winning figure was 7 points higher." So most of the winners had shown improvement from their previous race. Another study of 400 entrants in California in 1994, by Mark Cramer, found that, even for horses who were running back at the same distance and on the same surface and were not coming off layoffs, the average change, plus or minus, was 10.9 Beyer points from the last race. In addition, Cramer discovered that "Only 30 percent of the entrants ran within two lengths of their last race."

   Based on this kind of evidence, the most valuable approach to picking winners should not rely on horses that have just run a big race, although at least some of them will still be able to run even better next time out. Rather, the most valuable approach is to try to project a horse's future improvement. Easier said than done, I know, but that's what much of the rest of this book will be aiming to do.

2. Top Beyer figures seldom go off at big odds. A big percentage of them are favorites or second choices. Because it relies so heavily on the most recent past-performance line, keying on the top Beyer figure represents a more static approach to handicapping. By way of contrast, a more dynamic approach tries to anticipate change and improvement. It is more in tune with the often changeable, even erratic nature of Thoroughbred behavior, and it tends to go deeper into the horse's past performances, looking for revealing patterns that form over time. And it's where the value lies.

So, if you're looking for better odds, it makes more sense to see the top figure as a target to be attacked (when sensible, of course), rather than a horse to be bet—which leads us to that most pervasive but poorly understood concept in modern handicapping: the bounce.

BEYER BOUNCERS

OUR LANGUAGE IS a living thing. Words continually appear and disappear over time. As the generations pass, new expressions come into general use while others fade into oblivion. It's a fascinating study. But you don't need to be a linguist or a lexicographer to trace these changes in our language. All you have to do is take a walk through your local racetrack or simulcast center and listen to the handicappers talk.

Ten or 15 years ago, if you had heard someone say that a horse was going to "bounce," you would have scratched your head, looked at him strangely, and questioned the wisdom of his being at the racetrack—or even out on the streets at all. But today the word has come into common usage at the races. We all know what it means. At least I *think* we all know what it means.

Back in the 1950's and 1960's, a New Yorker named Len Ragozin began to develop and market a set of speed figures under the trade name The Sheets. It has since cultivated a wide appeal among a select group of horseplayers, many of whom are substantial bettors. In that way Ragozin's product, and offshoots like Jerry Brown's Thoro-Graph, have introduced a number of key concepts now commonly used in analyzing speed figures, and they continue to have a sizable influence on the odds at many racetracks. One of Ragozin's concepts was the bounce.

This relatively new word emphasizes something that we have known about for many years but that we used to describe in different terms. Some called it a *form cycle*, while others used phrases such as *muscle sore*. But with the advent of Len Ragozin and The Sheets, the term *bounce* sought to give greater sophistication and precision to such indistinct concepts, and the term has since trickled down to the rest of us.

What exactly does it mean when we say a horse bounced? The most accurate definition goes something like this: A horse bounces, or reacts, because he has exhausted himself in one or more extremely stressful efforts. Horses that have drained themselves in this way will run substantially worse in their next race, or races, and will need time to recover before they can return to that earlier "peak" of performance. Of course, there has never been a theory that works 100 percent of the time at the races—or even 80 percent or 60 percent of the time—and not every horse bounces the way he is supposed to, according to the theory. But, since it is grounded in the undeniable impact of exhausting efforts on the physical energy and fitness of the Thoroughbred, there is a great deal of merit in the theory. It is logical, it makes sense, and, to a valuable extent, it works.

Just as with many other words that originally had a limited, more targeted definition, the meaning of the term *bounce* has shifted and broadened as it has achieved more common, widespread usage. Too many people now use the term to describe any horse that runs worse in his next race—not just those that were reacting to peak efforts or unusually stressful performances. That sort of stretching or blurring of the definition can be troublesome. For example, if a horse encounters ideal or exceptional circumstances in his previous race—if he is the lone speed, or runs on a wet track, or gets an absolutely perfect trip—you would expect him to run a lower figure next time out when he is no longer favored by those ideal conditions. Since the horse might not have experienced any kind of excessive stress, the decline in his figures probably should not be called a bounce. Yet many of us have taken to using the word in this broader sense. If you are going to use the concept of a bounce in your handicapping, you need to understand this distinction between the narrower and broader definitions.

Take the case of Gold Oxide.

2	**Gold Oxide**											

Past performance chart for Gold Oxide. Own: Paraneck Stable. Black Cherry Ball. CHAVEZ J F (69 9 13 9 .13) 2002:(1129 209 .19). B. f. 3 (May) EASOCT00 $35,000. Sire: Gold Fever (Forty Niner) $5,000. Dam: Zinc Oxide (Sun Master). Br: Questroyal 100 LLC (NY). Tr: Pedersen Jennifer (26 2 1 3 .08) 2002:(138 13 .09). $70,000. L 116.

	Life	8 2 2 0	$76,880	90	D.Fst	6 0 2 0	$24,080	58
	2002	8 2 2 0	$76,880	90	Wet(316)	2 2 0 0	$52,800	90
	2001	0 M 0 0	$0	–	Turf(275*)	0 0 0 0	$0	–
	Aqu	2 0 1 0	$9,610	58	Dst(345)	5 2 2 0	$70,610	90

30Oct02–7Aqu fst 6f	:22^2 :46 :58^3 1:10^3 3↑⑥⑤Alw 47000N2x	58 3 5	2^{hd} 2^{hd} 4^3 5^{10}	Chavez J F	L 120 fb	2.45	74 – 16	GrbBg120$^{3\frac{3}{4}}$ JezbelCntSpell120$^{2\frac{1}{4}}$ KrkorumCrusder120$^{1\frac{3}{4}}$	Vied outside, tired 7
11Oct02–7Bel sly 6f	:22^3 :46^1 :58^3 1:11^2 3↑⑥⑤Alw 45000N1x	90 3 8	1$^{1\frac{1}{2}}$ 1^3 1^8 1$^{13\frac{1}{4}}$	Chavez J F	L 119 fb	*1.25	81 – 25	GoldOxide119^{13} StreetWheling117$^{3\frac{1}{4}}$ LvltToBtsy119$^{\frac{1}{4}}$	Set pace, ridden out 8
28Sep02–1Bel my 6f	:22^3 :46 :58 1:10^4 3↑⑥⑤Md Sp Wt 43k	58 3 10	3$^{1\frac{1}{2}}$ 3$^{1\frac{1}{2}}$ 3$^{\frac{1}{2}}$ 1$^{\frac{3}{4}}$	Chavez J F	L 118 fb	2.05e	84 – 11	GoldOxide118$^{\frac{3}{4}}$ TuftOfFlowrs118$^{\frac{1}{2}}$ SunstionJuli118^5	Got through on rail 10
19Sep02–1Bel fst 7f	:23^1 :47 1:13 1:26^2 3↑⑥⑤Md Sp Wt 43k	48 10 9	5$^{1\frac{1}{4}}$ 3^{nk} 2$^{3\frac{1}{2}}$ 4$^{4\frac{1}{4}}$	Luzzi M J	L 120 fb	4.50	67 – 20	My Girl Nessa120^4 Irish Rail120^{nk} Lady Nelson120^{no}	4 wide trip, no rally 12
1Sep02–2Sar fst 6f	:23^1 :47^2 1:00^2 1:14 3↑⑥⑤Md Sp Wt 41k	48 13 4	3$^{\frac{1}{2}}$ 2^{hd} 2^{hd} 2$^{\frac{3}{4}}$	Arroyo N Jr	L 118 fb	5.80	71 – 15	Budapest Girl118$^{\frac{3}{4}}$ Gold Oxide118$^{2\frac{3}{4}}$ DeadOfWinter118$^{2\frac{3}{4}}$	Pace, outfinished 13
23Aug02–1Sar fst 7f	:22^4 :46^3 1:12^2 1:25 3↑⑥⑤Md Sp Wt 41k	39 4 8	1$^{1\frac{1}{2}}$ 1^2 2^6 5$^{16\frac{1}{2}}$	Wynter N A	L 119 b	5.50	63 – 14	Grab Bag119^{10} Winloc's Sunshine119$^{3\frac{1}{2}}$ Pocahaba119$^{1\frac{1}{2}}$	Set pace, tired 12
	Previously trained by Aquilino Joseph								
19May02–2Bel fst 7f	:23^1 :47^2 1:13 1:25^4 3↑⑥⑤Md Sp Wt 41k	55 7 12	7$^{2\frac{3}{4}}$ 6$^{2\frac{1}{2}}$ 3$^{3\frac{1}{2}}$ 4$^{3\frac{1}{2}}$	Arroyo N Jr	L 116	2.10	70 – 14	AngelOfTheSe123$^{\frac{1}{2}}$ CughtChtin*116^{nk} JtSLizz116^{no}	Between foes, no rally 13
4May02–3Aqu fst 6f	:22^4 :46^2 :59^3 1:13^1 3↑⑥⑤Md Sp Wt 41k	47 7 8	6$^{6\frac{1}{2}}$ 5^3 3$^{4\frac{1}{2}}$ 2$^{3\frac{1}{2}}$	Arroyo N Jr	115	*2.65	68 – 25	SltrssOfSwng123$^{3\frac{1}{2}}$ GoldOxd115^{nk} BlondDynmt115$^{3\frac{1}{2}}$	Veered out, veered in 8

WORKS: ●Sep12 Aqu 5f fst 1:02^2 B *1/10* ●Aug21 Aqu 4f fst :47^1 H *1/5*
TRAINER: Dirt(133 .11 $2.46) Sprint(104 .13 $2.18) Claim(13 .08 $0.58)

In his race on October 11, Gold Oxide jumped up explosively from very ordinary Beyers of 48 and 58 all the way to a 90. You could hardly have anticipated such a huge increase, but it's easily explainable with hindsight. Gold Oxide had a clear lead on a sloppy track and ran big. It happens all the time. When, in his next start, they took away his sloppy track and his easy lead, Gold Oxide ran a whole lot worse, and at odds of 2-1. Did he bounce? If you think that the mere fact of such a dramatic increase in his Beyers constituted excessive stress, then perhaps you could say he bounced. But the trip did not appear particularly stressful. He wasn't challenged. He wasn't dueling. He wasn't going head and head for an extended distance. And he wasn't punished all the way to the wire.

In contrast to Gold Oxide, Obligation North's race on August 2 fits all the major categories of a strict definition of a bounce.

7 Obligation North
Own:Cronauer Bruce W
Yellow, Purple Sash
CARMOUCHE K (4 0 1 0 .00) 2002:(743 82 .11)

B. f. 3 (Feb) EASFEB00 $2,700
Sire: Valley Crossing (Private Account) $2,000
Dam: Turning North(Obligato)
Br: Martin Fallon (Pa)
Tr: Jeannont Diane (—) 2002:(63 3 .05)

L 117

Life	12	3	1	2	$36,325	62	D.Fst 11 3 1 2 $36,325 62
2002	12	3	1	2	$36,325	62	Wet(335) 1 0 0 0 $0 26
2001	0	M	0	0	$0	–	Turf(220) 0 0 0 0 $0 –
Del	4	1	0	1	$12,330	61	Dst(310) 8 2 1 2 $26,045 62

18Aug02-5Del fst 6f :22 :451 :582 1:114 ⒻClm c-(12.5-10.5) 56 3 2 44 57½ 49 312¼ Johnston M T L 119 b 3.90 72-19 CnbyDncr11910 CountThStrs1171½ ObligtonNorth119½ Mild rally for show 6
Claimed from Gill Michael J for $12,500, Robb John J Trainer 2002(as of 08/18): (416 66 68 54 0.16)
2Aug02-2Lrl fst 6f :231 :472 :593 1:12 3↑ⒻClm 15000(15-12)N3L 62 3 4 31 21 2hd 1hd Johnston M T L 114 b 5.20 79-20 ObligtionNorth114hd Poched1173¾ MyDrDolly1171¾ Rated 3-4w,bid,driving 8
23Jly02-4Del fst 5f :214 :462 :593 3↑ⒻClm 10000(10-9)N2L 61 4 1 61½ 41¾ 32 12½ Johnston M T L 114 b 22.20 88-17 *OblgtonNorth*1142½ MdmKppr108hd FrnchFctor1182¾ Closed outside, clear 8
7Jly02-5Del fst 6f :214 :451 :581 1:121 3↑ⒻClm 10000(10-9)N2L 40 2 5 43 45¼ 516 816¾ Johnston M T L 114 b 8.40 65-18 *JstCllMBrty*11811 [DH]JwlAlrm115 [DH]FrnchFctor118¾ Through after half 11
23Jun02-8Del fst 6f :221 :462 :592 1:123 3↑ⒻClm 25000(25-20)N2L 40 7 1 22½ 42½ 58 514 McCarthy M J L 114 b 8.90 66-22 Interlude1143¼ Piccolo Honey1165¾ *Bella Diablo*1153¾ Tired 7
6Jun02-4Pim fst 1 1/16 :24 :48 1:14 1:474 ⒻAlw 26000N1X 17 2 12 12½ 1hd 515 535¾ Pino M G L 117 b 19.00 32-32 Tamayo1174¾ Glorious Cat1173¾ Beauty's Image1178½ Rail, faltered, eased 6
22May02-6Pim fst 6f :233 :472 1:003 1:134 ⒻAlw 26000N1X 22 7 1 1hd 21½ 75¾ 713¼ Rocco J L 117 b 9.10 63-23 HolyMnd1172½ BrcngBty1221¾ TwoFromThBls117no 3wd 1/2,press 2w,tired 7
25Apr02-8Pim fst 6f :232 :47 :594 1:131 3↑ⒻMd c-(25-20) 55 7 1 1hd 13½ 15 17¼ Dominguez R A L 115 b *2.10 79-17 OblgtonNorth1157¼ LdyZomZm1222¾ SstyAnn110¾ Rail,drew off,rddn out 9
Claimed from Team 26 for $25,000, Feliciano Ben M Jr Trainer 2002(as of 04/25): (102 14 17 18 0.14)
17Mar02-5CT my 4½f :224 :472 :534 ⒻMd Sp Wt 16k 26 5 9 75¾ 77¾ 78 Pindell M D L 119 b *1.00 74-17 Alley Ack1192 Pleasant Hope1194¼ Valet Girl119nk 4 wide turn 10
27Feb02-4Lrl fst 1 1/16 :24 :48 1:122 1:451 ⒻMd Sp Wt 25k 8 6 22 21½ 36 524 642¼ Johnston M T L 122 b *2.50 41-24 Tmyo12219 FreedomOfPort122no Dorothy'sWgr1228¾ Stalked 2wd, faltered 7
WORKS: Sep13 Pha 4f fst :481 B *3/11*
TRAINER: 1stClaim(7 .14 $1.37) Dirt(129 .08 $1.59) Sprint(84 .07 $1.90) Alw(35 .06 $0.33)

It was a lifetime-best figure for the filly. It came after a substantial improvement from much poorer figures. And it was earned under very stressful conditions, chasing and dueling three- and four- wide, and battling head and head in a stiff drive through the entire stretch. In her next race Obligation North could only manage a third-place finish and a Beyer of 56.

Perhaps this is a distinction without a difference—at least for parimutuel purposes. Perhaps we need not be bothered fretting over "performance" bounces versus some other sort of simple decline in a horse's speed figures due to an obvious change in racing conditions and circumstances. Still, I do think it's worth keeping in mind. On some occasions this distinction will make a difference in your handicapping.

If you accept the validity of the concept of a bounce—however narrowly or broadly defined—you should not take this as an invitation to bet against every top Beyer Speed Figure in every race. As always, any big figure has to be seen in the context of the overall record of any particular horse—as part of a pattern of figures over time. But if a horse has some of the more obvious features of a bounce candidate, it's worth being skeptical about that horse's chances. While these horses don't always bounce when the theory says they should, thinking skeptically about these peak efforts can be a valuable weapon in the never-ending battle to get value at the windows.

In fact, in my view, using the Beyer figures to help identify potential bouncers is absolutely essential to any successful betting strategy. Any time you can throw out an "obvious" 8-5 shot, or a 3-5 favorite who might bounce after a peak effort, you're sitting on a potential score. And, after all, without those occasional big pay-days, in the long run we'd all be ground down to dust.

Since the bounce is such a valuable handicapping and betting tool, it is worth exploring potential bouncers in much greater depth. Unfortunately, the guidelines are many, they are complicated, and they are controversial. If you want to understand just how difficult these guidelines can be, just take a look at Len Ragozin's 1997 book, *The Odds Must Be Crazy*. The man who introduced all of us to the "bounce" argues that there is nothing simple about it, that it is in no way cut-and-dried. In fact, he stresses that it is more a matter of "likelihoods" and "percentages" than of certainties and guarantees. And the likelihood of a horse bouncing will vary according to a list of factors—a daunting and distressingly long list of factors:

1. **Size of the jump from previous race.** The larger the jump from the previous speed figure to the peak figure, the more likely it is that a horse will react. The more gradual the improvement, the less likely he is to bounce.

2. **Running styles.** Speed horses, especially those who had to battle hard on the lead, are more likely to bounce than come-from-behind runners. Front-runners appear to be more severely affected by excessive stress.

3. **Sprinter or router.** Sprinters are more likely to bounce than routers.

4. **Type of race.** The cheaper the race, and the cheaper the horse, the more likely it is that the horse will not be able to stand up to a peak performance.

5. **Sex.** Fillies and mares are more likely to bounce than colts and geldings.

6. **Age.** Older horses are more likely to suffer a setback after an unusually big effort.

7. **Grass or dirt.** Turf runners are less prone to a bounce than dirt runners. Grass figures are generally more consistent, with fewer dramatic increases and decreases.

8. **Physical soundness.** Horses with big gaps in their form indicating severe and recurring physical problems are more likely candidates for a bounce.

9. **Trainer skills.** Horses are more likely to bounce if they are in the hands of less competent trainers. The more talented and conscientious the trainer, the less likely the bounce.

10. **Recency of race.** If a horse has been rested for a substantial period of time since his peak performance, and thus given more of a chance to recover, he is less likely to bounce. If he comes back within a week or two of his big effort, he is more likely to bounce.

excellent race + rest time is good

11. **Number of races.** The more races a horse has run in the very recent past, the more likely he is to bounce.

12. **Frequency of races.** The more space between a horse's races—though not the huge gaps that often indicate unsoundness—the fresher he will be, and so the less likely it is that he will bounce.

As if these complications and qualifications were not enough, all these considerations fail to confront what is perhaps the most critical judgment of all—not merely deciding whether a horse will bounce, but how badly. As we shall see, this judgment is vitally important. But Ragozin is similarly careful and cautious on this subject. When trying to determine the size of any potential bounce, he writes, "There is no uniform answer." He merely suggests that the biggest bounce will come from a horse whose peak performance is completely "out of whack" with that horse's more typical performance—a horse such as the aforementioned Gold Oxide. The size of bounces and explosions, Ragozin tells us, is "really not predictable." All you can say for certain is that a horse is more likely to bounce, or less likely, according to the lengthy laundry list of criteria outlined above.

Before we allow the popularizer of bounce theory to qualify and modify his own creation completely out of existence, we need to step in here and reassert the usefulness of the concept, and its critical role in finding value. Let's start with a simple question: How can you recognize a potential bounce? Since we can't define it with any certainty or specificity, and the guidelines are unwieldy, we'll have to fall back on some classic examples. As the judge said in a very different context, you might not be able to define it, but you'll know it when you see it.

1. Long layoff, big bounce. When a horse earns a huge Beyer or runs a very stressful race after a substantial layoff, you should be very skeptical about that horse's chances in his next race.

NO Good
long lay off
then
excellent race

On August 1 Sejm's Madness was all out, every step of the way, at an extended distance. And he ran a very big Beyer. Four weeks later he returned to the races and couldn't keep up at all. His Beyer plunged to a 47. Of course, not every horse with this profile will react the same way, but this category could perhaps be described as Most Likely to Bounce.

Two-year-olds returning to the races after a long layoff should be considered in a separate category. For example, if a horse runs figures of 50 and 55 as a 2-year-old and then comes back after a six-month layoff and runs a 67, that might simply qualify as normal improvement with maturity, rather than as an indication of a new top.

2. **Big jump to big Beyer.** The example of Mint Money makes the case with a vengeance.

```
6 Mint Money                                          B. c. 3 (Apr) OBSAPR01 $50,000                             Life  13 2 2 0  $22,420 79  D.Fst      12 1 2 0  $14,020 79
  Own:C D & G Stable                                  Sire: Jeblar (Alydar) $2,500                               2002  13 2 2 0  $22,420 79  Wet(325)    1 1 0 0   $8,400 73
  Turquoise, Black Diamond Belt, Black       $6,250   Dam: Minted(Key to the Mint)                       L 119   2001   0 M 0 0       $0  -  Turf(305)   0 0 0 0       $0  -
NELSON D (4 2 1 1 .50) 2002:(123 14 .11)              Br:  Farnsworth Farms (Fla)                                Med    1 1 0 0   $5,400 79  Dst(335)    8 1 1 0  $11,180 79
                                                      Tr:  Klesaris Robert P(13 2 1 4 .15) 2002:(277 31 .11)

25Sep02-5Del  fst 6f   :222 :463 :594 1:131     Clm 12500(12.5-10.5)     36 3 2  2½  32  4¾  812½ Coa E M        L117   3.00  64-14 Lothar1171¾ Moonmon1171¼ Angelic Hero1171½             Bid, faltered 10
10Sep02-6Med  fst 6f   :222 :444 :563 1:09   3↑ Clm 10000(10-9)N2L   79 10 1  1hd 11  13  12¾  Nelson D       L118   5.10  94-13 MintMoney1182¾ Romancer1223¾ WasAPoorMn1181   Pace,off rail,driving 10
27Aug02-6Pha  fst 5½f  :221 :453 :58  1:043 3↑ Clm 15000(15-13)N2L  -0 1 7  1hd 43  815 828¾ Arroyo E N5    L112   6.90  61-20 Bushy's Jay1207¼ No More Rummies1181¾ Kattalk1161¾           Used up 8
28Jly02-1Sar  fst 6½f  :222 :46  1:121 1:19     Clm 25000                32 8 2  1½  1hd 75¾ 915¾ Prado E S      L119  16.40  64-14 Mister Silence119no Megaluno121hd Hideaway Cafe119hd  Vied inside, tired 9
13Jly02-2Bel  fst 6f   :222 :46  :582 1:112     Clm 18500(22.5-18.5)     44 2 3  54¼ 42½ 57  513  Gryder A T     L115 *2.40e 68-20 SmrtTp116hd AllGeredUp117¾ Herecomsthwrdn1148     Chased inside, tired 7
 1Jly02-4Del  fst 6f   :222 :461 :592 1:13      Clm 12500(12.5-10.5)     67 4 2  2hd 1hd 13  21   Martin E M Jr  L117f  3.90  77-16 Deserving1171 MintMoney1171½ FreddiFrlodr117½   Vied,clear,not enough 7
17May02-2Bel  fst 6f   :224 :453 :573 1:10      Clm 20000                39 2 1  1hd 22  47  617  Nelson D       L117   3.80  71-14 Peggys Mukora1095½ Knight At Rao's1141¾ Wild Lu1175½  Tired after a half 6
13Apr02-2GP   fst 6f   :221 :451 :574 1:112     Clm c-(30-25)N2L         41 6 2  2hd 31  44½ 712½ Velasquez C    L122   *.80  69-16 ExtraValue1222½ FortunateRoyl1221 Jimmielee1222¼ Vied 3 wide, faltered 7
   Claimed from Meltzer Elaine J for $30,000, Plesa Edward Jr Trainer 2002(as of 04/13): ( 92 7 11 13 0.08 )
27Mar02-9GP   fst 6½f  :224 :454 1:111 1:181     Clm 30000(30-25)N2L      75 3 4  1hd 1hd 1hd 2hd  Velasquez C    L122   3.40  85-15 Dr. Can Do120hd Mint Money1221¾ Gray Forum1223½     Vied, just failed 10
15Mar02-6GP   fst 6f   :22  :45  :573 1:104     Clm 50000(50-45)         46 4 3  11  1hd 32  811½ Velasquez C    L120   9.30  73-11 SomeOthrNight118¾ LstIntntion1201 SlickrThnSlt120nk   On rail, faltered 8
WORKS: Aug24 Bel tr.t 5f fst 1:034 B 18/22  Aug15 Bel tr.t 4f fst :492 B 7/20
TRAINER: Dirt(607 .15 $1.37) Sprint(386 .15 $1.47) Claim(431 .15 $1.27)
```

That huge leap up to a 79 Beyer was followed two weeks later by a huge collapse down to a 36.

```
9 Crafty Account                                      B. c. 3 (Feb) OBSAPR01 $14,000                             Life  23 1 7 3  $30,360 73  D.Fst      21 1 7 2  $29,030 73
  Own:Hollows Lane                                    Sire: Top Account (Private Account) $3,000                 2002  17 1 5 2  $24,170 73  Wet(342)    2 0 0 1   $1,330 55
  Red, Gold Braces & S, Gold Stripes        $10,000   Dam: Crafty Melody(Crafty Prospector)              L 119   2001   6 M 2 1   $6,190 51  Turf(238)   0 0 0 0       $0  -
BEASLEY J A (54 8 4 6 .15) 2002:(554 58 .10)          Br:  Bruce Gibbs (Fla)                                     Crc   17 1 3 2  $17,940 73  Dst(245*)   9 0 3 0   $8,930 73
                                                      Tr:  Chavez Jesus(9 0 1 2 .00) 2002:(94 14 .15)

21Oct02-2Crc  fst 6½f  :224 :464 1:132 1:201 3↑ Clm c-(10-9)N2L       53 3 3  51¾ 52½ 42  53   Aguilar M         L118b  2.60  79-20 BiscayAppel118nk AvidDvid118½ Crypto'sKnight1181½   Stdy bkstr, no rally 8
   Claimed from Speiser Jane for $10,000, Hemmerick Anthony J Trainer 2002(as of 10/21): ( 44 3 6 10 0.07 )
 7Oct02-4Crc  fst 7f   :223 :46  1:112 1:244 3↑ Clm 10000(10-9)N2L    73 4 1  31½ 51¾ 24  21½  Aguilar M         L118b  5.80  88-14 SlyTruth1181½ CrftyAccount1187 NookiBooki1114  Steadied bkstr & turn 7
29Sep02-4Crc  gd  11/16 :241 :483 1:142 1:484 3↑ Clm 10000(10-9)N2L    55 7 42 31  3½  33  38¾  Aguilar M         L118b 10.00  59-24 Combine118¾ Cued Up1098 Crafty Account118nk          3 wide move, tired 9
14Sep02-8Crc  fst 7f   :223 :46  1:12  1:253 3↑ Clm 10000(10-9)N2L    54 3 5  31½ 21½ 43½ 49   Nunez E O         L118b 30.20  77-18 Alarm The C.E.O.1134¼ GloryD'or1221 BigFrank1183¾ Steadied chute, tired 8
 3Aug02-7Crc  fst 6f   :224 :47  :594 1:124 3↑ Clm 10000(10-9)N2L    45 5 3  2hd 31  64½ 710½ Boulanger G       L117b 34.90  69-15 PrinceForever1173 Tweenthlins1171 GloryD'or122¾  Vied inside, faltered 12
20Jly02-7Crc  fst 7f   :221 :452 1:121 1:27  3↑ Clm 10000(10-9)N2L    57 2 8  87¼ 78  54  54   Homeister R B Jr  L117   6.00  75-14 ProspectLne1221 Tweenthelines1171 ElNinoClint122¾     No late response 11
 1Jly02-5Crc  sly 6½f  :23  :471 1:13  1:193    Clm 16000(16-14)       52 4 5  73¾ 72  65  59   Homeister R B Jr  L119   9.10  76-14 Jaclini1172¾ So Nasty1191¾ Tough Exercise1123¾        5 wide, no threat 7
17Jun02-3Crc  fst 6½f  :232 :472 1:123 1:192 3↑ Md 16000(16-14)       64 6 1  52¾ 3nk 1½  1no  Homeister R B Jr  L117   3.20  86-13 Crafty Account117no Stacker1222½ River Reed1172    Bumped start, lasted 6
 7Jun02-10Crc fst 1    :241 :49  1:151 1:431    Md 16000(16-14)       34 9 65 74¼ 54½ 67  614  Aguilar M         L118  *1.90  51-30 AngelApproval116nk Nathan'sWy1185½ Gtorzone1181  Steadied bkstr, tired 9
24May02-2Crc  fst 1    :252 :494 1:16  1:432    Md 25000(25-22.5)     12 5 2hd 1hd 63½ 610 625½ Rivera J A II     L118   2.10  38-34 Oblong1181¾ VagueHint1092¾ BelieveICanFly1135¼ Bumped 1st turn, faded 7
WORKS: Nov9 Crc 5f fst 1:043 B 34/50  Oct19 Crc 3f fst :383 B 24/32  Sep12 Crc 3f gd :38 B (d)9/10  Aug18 Crc 4f fst :532 B 42/42
TRAINER: 1stClaim(4 .50 $19.70) Dirt(150 .13 $2.13) Sprint(110 .12 $2.34) Claim(60 .18 $2.27)
```

Crafty Account is a somewhat less dramatic example. After her sudden improvement by 18 points on October 7—up to a new lifetime best—she made a mini-move on the turn and then ran very flat through the stretch on October 21. That's the way many horses are affected by an overly stressful effort in the previous race. They're a bit sluggish. They simply can't muster the same peak level of energy. Crafty Account's Beyer fell to 53.

1 Galloping Dancer
Own:Kenline Stables
Yellow, Yellow Bars On Turquoise Sleeves
JOHNSTON M T (295 42 40 37 .14) 2002:(1014 156 .15)

B. f. 2 (Mar) OBSMAR02 $18,000
Sire: Cherokee Run (Runaway Groom) $20,000
Dam: Sefas Royal Dancer(Gate Dancer)
Br: Hindman Limited Partnership LLLP (Ky)
Tr: Lebarron Keith W(2 0 1 0 .00) 2002:(122 16 .13)

115

Life	6	1	0	3	$18,990	63	D.Fst	5	1	0	3	$17,850	63
2002	6	1	0	3	$18,990	63	Wet(435)	1	0	0	0	$1,140	28
2001	0	M	0	0	$0	–	Turf(195)	0	0	0	0	$0	–
Del	0	0	0	0	$0	–	Dst(290)	0	0	0	0	$0	–

31Aug02-4Pha	fst	6f	:214 :451 :581 1:122	ⒻAlw 24800N1X	40	6	1	54½	67	69½	39	Velazquez D C	118	4.50	68-12	Lghtnngnthr1158¾ Shlvsmtblls115hd GllpngDncr1181¾	Very wide, no factor	6
11Aug02-3Pha	fst	5½f	:22 :454 :592 1:063	ⒻMd Sp Wt 19k	63	9	4	75½	56½	26	12¼	Velazquez D C	118	13.00	80-20	GllopingDncer1182¼ *SeekingThSilvr*1188½ *Eliz'sCt*1182¼	Came5w,full of run	11
31Jly02-3Mth	fst	5½f	:224 :471 :593 1:061	ⒻMd 35000(35-30)	34	6	1	74	64¼	44	36½	Velazquez D C	117	7.30	79-16	She'sTheTicket1174 PiercedNvl1152½ *GllopingDncr*1171¾	5-wide into lane	7
10Jly02-1Mth	fst	5f	:23 :471 1:00	ⒻMd 35000(35-30)	33	1	4	63½	76¼	56¼	35¾	Rosado R J	117	15.10	74-20	EbonyPost1152½ *Shelovesmetblls*1173¼ GllopingDncer117½	Some late gain	8
29Jun02-4Pha	fst	4½f	:222 :46 :522	ⒻMd Sp Wt 25k	22	10	10	79		611	513	Rosado R J	118	10.30	83-16	*Lightningintheair*1184½ Trijonia118no Shelovesmetblls1181¾	Off slow, wide	10
15Jun02-1Pha	my	4½f	:23 :47 :532	ⒻMd Sp Wt 21k	28	6	7	54½		56	45	Rosado R J	118	3.40	86-13	Friel's For Real118no Trijonia1184 Tri This Way1181	No factor	7

TRAINER: 2YO(10 .20 $3.70) Sprint/Route(24 .17 $1.13) Dirt(252 .17 $1.53) Alw(87 .13 $0.97)

Galloping Dancer seemed to benefit from the switch from Monmouth to Philadelphia, but, after her 29-point improvement, she fell back to a 40.

3. **Back-to-back big Beyers.** If a horse does not bounce after one huge effort, then he is much more likely to bounce after a second one. Boston Common was a classic case.

9 Boston Common
Own:Englander Richard A
Green White Diamond Gray Sleeves
DOUGLAS R R (633 165 113 78 .26) 2002:(1121 223 .20)

B. c. 3 (Apr)
Sire: Boston Harbor (Capote) $23,000
Dam: Especially(Mr. Prospector)
Br: Overbrook Farm (Ky)
Tr: Pino Michael V (—) 2002:(309 79 .26)

L 122

Life	17	5	6	4	$361,427	107	D.Fst	15	5	5	3	$318,677	107
2002	11	3	4	2	$303,177	107	Wet(340)	2	0	1	1	$42,750	106
2001	6	2	2	2	$58,250	92	Turf(252)	0	0	0	0	$0	–
AP Ⓣ	0	0	0	0	$0	–	DstⓉ(310*)	0	0	0	0	$0	–

5Oct02-9Pha	fst	6f	:213 :441 :562 1:094	GallantBobH150k	96	2	2	1hd	2hd	2½	21½	Martin E M Jr	L 122	*.70	88-15	Thunderello1151½ Boston Common1226 Calends116hd	Dueled,rail, 2nd best	5
14Sep02-8Bel	fst	1	:231 :461 1:104 1:36	Jerome H-G2	107	7	11	11	11½	16	15	Chavez J F	L 118	2.35	89-15	BostonCommon1185 Vinemeistr1155½ NoProl115nk	Stumble start, driving	7
24Aug02-9Sar	sly	7f	:221 :444 1:094 1:224	KingsBishop-G1	106	4	3	1hd	1½	2hd	23	Chavez J F	L 121	13.70	88-17	Gygistar1243 *BostonCommon*1219 ThunderDys1151¼	Vied inside, gamely	8
3Aug02-8Sar	fst	6f	:214 :443 :564 1:092	Amsterdam-G2	92	7	1	2hd	1hd	13½	22¼	Prado E S	L 123	13.50	93-10	ListenHere1212¼ BostonCommon1233¼ BoldTruth115¾	Vied, clear, gamely	8
4Jly02-9Mth	fst	6f	:214 :443 :564 1:091	JerseyShore-G3	103	1	2	1½	1½	14½	12¾	Martin E M Jr	L 117	10.00	93-14	BostonCommon1172¾ *LstnHr*1173 It'sAMnstr1153	Pace,inside,clear,drvg	6
10Jun02-7Del	fst	6f	:221 :451 :572 1:094	Oh Say57k	82	3	1	11	2hd	2hd	37½	Martin E M Jr	L 119	1.40	86-09	It'sAMonstr1192 KntckyMd1175½ *BostonCommon*1196¼	Dueled, gave way	5
25May02-7Del	fst	6f	:213 :444 :58 1:11	Legal Light75k	95	4	1	2hd	2½	2hd	21¾	Martin E M Jr	L 119	5.50	86-19	*Running Tide*1191¾ Boston Common1191¾ Calends1193	Vied,led,caught	7
Previously trained by Reavis Michael L																		
4May02-7Mnr	fst	6f	:214 :451 :574 1:103	Alw 41600NC	94	1	1	11	12	11	15½	Walker B J Jr	LB 114	1.80	86-18	BostonCommon1145½ PrsidntButlr11410 FirThFirm1173	Plenty left at rail	6
6Apr02-8Spt	fst	1⅛	:481 1:13 1:373 1:494	Ill Derby-G2	57	8	21½	42	65	816	833½	Emigh C A	L 114	135.10	58-17	*War Emblem*1146¼ Repent1244½ Fonz's1176½	Steady fade	9
17Mar02-8Spt	fst	1	:233 :47 1:122 1:391	Alw 48600NC	73	2	21	21½	21½	23	313¾	Sterling L J Jr	L 115	4.70	73-20	*WarEmblem*11810 *ColorfulTour*1213 BostonCommon1158	Lost place late	6
11Mar02-8Spt	fst	1	:241 :48 1:124 1:38	3↑ Alw 32000N2X	75	8	11½	12½	12	1hd	45½	Sterling L J Jr	L 114	*3.00	87-16	Robin Zee1131¾ Naskramoon119½ R. T. Gulch1193¼	Tired	9
Previously trained by Pino Michael V																		
8Dec01-8Hou	gd	7f	:221 :452 1:113 1:25	Alamo25k	67	5	1	1hd	1½	2hd	33½	Murphy B G	L 117	*.40	79-13	DustySpike1181 DeRIDI1172½ BostonCommon11711	Dueled, 2w, weakened	6
17Oct01-7Del	fst	6f	:221 :454 :582 1:112	Alw 32300N1X	92	1	3	11½	1hd	11½	12¼	Santiago J	L 117	*.50	86-26	BostonCommon1172¼ PrsdntBtlr1177¾ Fl'sB1122¾	Shown whip, ridden out	6
8Sep01-9Med	fst	6f	:212 :441 :562 1:093	Comet48k	80	2	1	23	21½	21	2½	Santiago J	L 116	2.10	90-10	FinlTbl116½ *BostonCommon*1166¾ WinningTlk11614	Carried out some late	4
19Aug01-5Del	fst	6f	:223 :463 :593 1:123	Md Sp Wt 32k	73	12	1	1½	1hd	1½	13¾	Santiago J	L 118	*1.40	80-20	Boston Common1183¾ MazoolianGhost1182½ Halo'sTiger1182¾	Clearly best	12
10Jly01-3Del	fst	5f	:213 :454 :583	Md Sp Wt 39k	61	2	2	42½	44	44	32¾	Black A S	L 117	*1.00	90-12	*Booklet*1171 Outathechute1171¾ *Boston Common*1172¼	Came out, gaining	9
23Jun01-1Del	fst	5f	:221 :461 :592	Md c-(50-45)	79	7	1	1½	1½	1hd	22¼	King E L Jr	117	3.20	87-17	RdThTgr1122¼ BostonCmmn1177½ QrtrTnOfFn1172	Dueled,hung,2nd best	8

Claimed from Overbrook Farm for $50,000, Lukas D Wayne Trainer 2001(as of 06/23): (375 51 52 49 0.14)
WORKS: Sep29 Pha 3f fst :361 B *5/10* Sep9 Del 3f fst :372 B *3/6* Aug18 Del 4f fst :502 B *8/18* Jly28 Del 4f fst :483 B *2/14*
TRAINER: 1stTurf(31 .10 $1.35) Sprint/Route(67 .10 $0.94) Turf(186 .17 $1.35) GrdStk(6 .33 $4.78)

At a much less exalted level, the very modest filly Mystic Crown provides another example—as does Ameri Brilliance.

2 Mystic Crown
Own:Souder Donald E
White, Red Horse, Red Sleeves, White Cap
TEATOR P A (10 0 3 0 .00) 2002:(553 50 .09)

$8,000

Ch. f. 3 (Mar) KEESEP00 $20,000
Sire: Twining (Forty Niner) $10,000
Dam: Half Crown(Key to the Mint)
Br: C E S Racing Ltd (Ky)
Tr: Souder Donald E(2 0 0 0 .00) 2002:(61 5 .08)

L 117

Life	25	2	7	2	$57,663	67	D.Fst	18	0	3	2	$15,933	52
2002	12	0	2	1	$9,753	52	Wet(385)	4	0	3	0	$12,330	67
2001	13	2	5	1	$47,910	67	Turf(235)	3	2	1	0	$29,400	55
Lrl	8	0	1	0	$4,560	39	Dst(345)	11	0	2	0	$10,680	67

9Oct02-5Lrl	fst	6f	:222 :461 :582 1:104	3↑ ⒻClm 12000(15-12)B	39	3	4	54½	64¾	58	512½	Kreidel K J	L 112 b	35.00	73-19	Sass Valay1167½ Aunt Celie109½ Balantrae119hd	Very wide, no rally	8
18Sep02-2Pim	fst	6f	:232 :463 :591 1:131	3↑ ⒻClm 7500(7.5-6.5)N3L	36	3	2	54¼	513	513	713	Kreidel K J	L 115 b	10.20	66-25	LdyZoomZoom1127½ FolsFllInLv1171¾ CntryJd1081	6wd upper, weakened	9
7Sep02-4Pim	fst	6f	:231 :463 :592 1:124	3↑ ⒻClm 13500(15-12)N3L	52	7	1	45	58½	75½	44½	Kreidel K J	L 113 b	54.60	77-20	RockFevr1192¾ Portntos112hd Stormin'Dorothy1101½	6-wide, flattened out	8
30Aug02-4Tim	fst	*6½f	:224 :48 1:133 1:184	3↑ ⒻClm 5000(5-4)N3L	51	7	6	44½	31½	32½	34¼	Kreidel K J	L 114 b	5.70	83-14	*LdyZoomZom*1123½ ErndlGld111¾ MystcCrwn1144½	3wd bid 1/4,outfinishd	9
23Aug02-1Lrl	fst	6f	:23 :471 1:00 1:124	3↑ ⒻClm 5000(5-4)N2Y	39	2	4	32	33	34	25¾	Kreidel K J	L 114 b	8.60	69-23	RestlssRuckus1175¾ MysticCrown114¾ SoSilvr1083	Bobbled start,willing	7
16Aug02-2Lrl	fst	6f	:222 :462 :583 1:111	3↑ ⒻClm 7500(7.5-6.5)N3L	13	5	2	3½	23	613	721¾	Goodwin N	L 115 b	2.50e	61-18	*Chlo'sQust*1126½ *Qustforcmlot*117no *NorthrnDlx*1105½	Hard used 3wd, tired	8
16Mar02-8CT	fst	6½f	:233 :474 1:143 1:214	ⒻClm 12500(12.5-10.5)N3L	31	2	3	66	87¼	78¾	613¾	Goodwin N	L 119 b	4.50	66-21	*Frecci*1163½ SewSnguSlw1194¾ SouthCountyLdy1113½	Force in bump turn	10
2Mar02-7CT	sly	7f	:24 :491 1:153 1:291	ⒻClm 12500(12.5-10.5)N3L	42	3	2	31½	42¼	36	210	Goodwin N	L 119 b	2.60	65-20	Cn'tStopSmokn11610 MystcCrown119¾ DoubtflGst1143	Second best late	10
15Feb02-1Lrl	fst	7f	:233 :474 1:14 1:273	ⒻClm 10000(10-9)	38	2	3	41½	42	32	44	Kreidel K J	L 117 b	11.70	65-23	EtrnlRgns117½ D KssnConcrn1121 CozyCn1172½	Saved ground, weakened	7
3Feb02-2Lrl	fst	6f	:223 :462 :593 1:132	ⒻClm 12500(12.5-10.5)	34	9	3	99½	910	78½	87	Kreidel K J	L 117 b	14.40	65-21	*Secret Expectation*1121 Trust Fund1173 I Do Declare1191	Outrun	9

WORKS: Aug10 Lrl 5f fst 1:01 H *4/21* Aug3 Lrl 4f fst :493 B *14/31* ●Jly29 Lrl 3f fst :37 B *1/5*
TRAINER: Dirt(150 .05 $0.46) Sprint(121 .07 $0.63) Claim(86 .01 $0.09)

1 Ameri Brilliance
Own:Bassford Elaine C
Peach, Brown Triangle, Brown Bars
FOGELSONGER R (75 21 8 10 .28) 2002:(853 181 .21)

B. c. 3 (Jan)
Sire: Ameri V: ay (Carnivalay) : 2,500
Dam: Seeking ·illiance(Seekin , the Gold)
Br: Marshele : Bassford Burgess (Md)
Tr: Leatherbury King T(15 3 1 6 .20) 2002:(255 35 .14)

L 113⁵

Life	10	3	1	1	$66,720	88
2002	6	2	0	1	$45,280	88
2001	4	1	1	0	$21,440	80
Lrl	4	1	0	1	$18,460	87

D.Fst	9	3	1	1	$66,720	88
Wet(285*)	0	0	0	0	$0	–
Turf(170*)	1	0	0	0	$0	23
Dst(275)	7	3	0	1	$62,310	88

9Oct02–7Lrl fst 7f :224 :46 1:11 1:231 3↑ OClm 30000(30–25)N **56** 2 2hd 1hd 42 713 Johnston M T L121 b *1.70 78–19 Polish Pride117¾ **Pipeline**119²¾ Poncho Duck117²½ Drifted 4wd 3/16,eased 7
24Sep02–6Del fst 6f :214 :452 :582 1:113 3↑ Alw 46300N2X **88** 1 1hd 1hd 11 12¼ Fogelsonger R5 L112 b 2.70 85–26 AmeriBrillinc112²¼ AccountForM1181 *Kingmkr*115¹¾ Got out turn, driving 6
22Aug02–6Lrl fst 6f :221 :451 :571 1:094 Alw 25480N1X **87** 4 3 3½ 1hd 13 13¾ Johnston M T L117 b 4.60 90–15 *AmeriBrillinc*117³¾ SunStorm119¾ PolishSon11710 Hard hld 3-4w,rddn out 5
9Aug02–6Lrl fst 6f :224 :461 :581 1:103 3↑ Alw 26000N1X **74** 2 7 77¼ 64½ 44 33 Johnston M T L114 b 10.00 83–18 Metro Time112²½ *Govans*117½ *AmeriBrilliance*114¾ Std'd st,5wd run,hung 7
25Jun02–7Cnl fm 5½f Ⓣ :23 :454 :573 1:034 3↑ Alw 26000N1X **23** 4 5 1hd 53 1019 1021½ Torres R5 L110 b 8.80 69–16 AccessAgnd117¹½ VictorySpin117¾ JustJustinin1155 2wd,dueled,faltered 11
16Jun02–6Pim fst 6f :23 :463 :592 1:123 3↑ Alw 26000N1X **36** 4 5 2½ 3½ 811 1019 Klinger C O L117 b 15.70 63–14 Bassous117½ Govans117no Metro Time117nk Pressed, faltered 10
26Oct01–6Lrl fst 6f :223 :461 :583 1:11 Alw 25480N1X **60** 4 5 53 51¾ 46 511½ Johnston M T L120 b 2.60 72–25 *Oswayo*120nk *President Butler*115⁵¾ Flo's Bo115⁵¼ Bobbld st,std'd 3-1/2 5
13Oct01–7Pim fst 6f :223 :451 :583 1:113 Ⓡ MdMllnNursry95k **50** 5 8 1hd 1½ 1hd 613 Torres R L120 b 2.70 75–10 Pl'sPrtnr1204 PrvtOpnng1152 SqrCtDmnd120²¾ Bumped start,2wd,tired 9
15Sep01–9Pim fst 6f :23 :463 :59 1:121 Md Sp Wt 25k **80** 11 1 15 16 16 17¼ Torres R7 L113 b *1.50 85–23 AmeriBrillince113⁷¼ Duvlier1201 PrivteOpening120nk Pace off rail, driving 12
3Sep01–5Tim fst 4f :221 :452 Md Sp Wt 21k **67** 8 6 33 22½ 22¾ Torres R7 113 b 12.20 95–06 *CoolCsh*115²¾ *AmeriBrillince*113³½ *InnrCommnd*120½ Drifted wide, rallied 10
WORKS: Sep21 Lrl 3f fst :37 B *8/17* ●Sep12 Lrl 5f fst 1:01 B *1/11* Sep7 Lrl 3f fst :38 B *6/15* Jly31 Lrl 4f fst :48 H *2/21* Jly27 Lrl 3f gd :392 B *4/4*
TRAINER: Dirt(599 .14 $1.43) Sprint(428 .13 $1.38) Alw(114 .12 $1.66)

When you hear a Sheets user referring to a "double top" or "pairing tops," this is the kind of pattern they are identifying.

4. **Three-and-out.** This phrase was coined by Andrew Beyer to describe a very specific phenomenon: When a horse has a sequence of three improving Beyer figures (such as 72-78-86, or 80-91-105), there is a substantial likelihood of that horse's running a lower Beyer next time. At Beyer's request, *Daily Racing Form* analyzed 4,518 horses that had just such a pattern of improving figures. Here were the results:

- 1,125 (25 percent) improved again in their next race
- 192 (4 percent) ran the same figure as in their previous start
- 3,201 (71 percent) declined in the next race
- 2,368 (52 percent) declined by six points or more

There are hundreds of examples of this pattern in every week's worth of races. Of course, not all of the 71 percent whose Beyers declined could be said to have bounced. Some only declined by a point or two. Others simply ran into difficulties with distance or class or track condition. But the fact that 52 percent declined by six points or more should put everyone on notice that this pattern needs to be identified and dealt with in any horse's past performances. The example of Will Of The Woods is as dramatic as you'll ever find:

1 Will Of The Woods
Own: Woods Clarence E
Peach, Emerald Green Belt, Green Band — $25,000
HUTTON G W (10 2 0 0 .20) 2002:(197 24 .12)

B. c. 3 (Mar)
Sire: Smelly (Judge Smells) $1,500
Dam: Willard's Peach(Willard Scott)
Br: Mary P Peach (Md)
Tr: Hairfield William E(1 0 0 0 .00) 2002:(22 1 .05)

L 118

Life	11	2	2	0	$32,520	81
2002	6	1	2	0	$21,060	81
2001	5	1	0	0	$11,460	44
Lrl	6	1	1	0	$16,950	58
D.Fst	9	2	1	0	$27,060	81
Wet(311)	2	0	1	0	$5,460	58
Turf(160*)	0	0	0	0	$0	–
Dst(310*)	1	0	0	0	$1,380	44

4Oct02-6Pim	fst	6f	:231 :454 :58 1:11	Alw 26000N1x	–0	5	7	31½	726	729	764½	Hutton G W	L 117 fb	10.10	25-17	Sun Storm1171¼ Cobbley Six1171¾ Tacirring1171¼	Taken up 3-1/2,eased	8
20Sep02-6Pim	fst	6f	:234 :464 :59 1:113 3↑	Clm 25000(25-20)N2L	81	4	4	11	12	17	18¾	Hutton G W	L 120 fb	*1.60	87-20	WllOfThWoods1208¾ Kmrton117½ *ChndlrCp*1221	2wd,mild hand pressure	7
5Sep02-4Pim	fst	6f	:24 :472 :592 1:13 3↑	Clm 25000(25-20)N2L	62	3	3	3nk	3½	23½	2¾	Douglas F G	L 120 b	5.20	79-20	TheDustmn122¾ *WillOfTheWoods*120¾ Lthimrun111nk	3-4wd trip, gamely	7
22Aug02-6Lrl	fst	6f	:221 :451 :571 1:094	Alw 25480N1x	50	1	4	2hd	31½	410	414½	Rosenthal M E	L 117 b	26.80	75-15	*AmeriBrilliance*1173¾ SunStorm119¾ PolishSon11710	Vied rail, tired upper	5
9Aug02-6Lrl	fst	6f	:224 :461 :581 1:103 3↑	Alw 26000N1x	55	5	2	31	2½	56½	710¾	Rosenthal M E	L 115 b	8.40	75-18	Metro Time1122½ *Govans*117½ *Ameri Brilliance*114¾	3wd,bid turn,tired	7
26Jly02-9Lrl	my	5½f ⊗	:23 :47 :594 1:063 3↑	Alw 26000N1x	58	6	5	42¼	32½	23	21½	Rosenthal M E	L 115 b	21.80	79-24	Jskprollnlong1141½ WllOfThWds1151¼ GldPrl1178¼	Circled, closed gamely	6
21Dec01-6Lrl	fst	7f	:23 :462 1:124 1:27	Clm 25000(25-20)	44	2	4	65¼	76½	65	45¼	Rosenthal M E	L 117 b	26.30	67-22	ExpctdColors1172¼ InfintSplndor115¾ SwpThShor1122¼	Rail trip, willingly	9
25Nov01-7Lrl	my	6f	:222 :462 :593 1:131	Alw 26000N1x	23	9	4	1½	56½	811	1018½	Douglas F G	L 117 b	58.40	54-27	*President Butler*1172 ***Proper Card***117no Miner Note1171¾	Dropped back	10
26Oct01-9Lrl	fst	6f	:221 :461 :594 1:141	Md 25000(25-20)	44	4	3	1hd	1hd	12	11¾	Rosenthal M E	L 120 b	7.30	68-25	WillOfThWoods1201¾ *WllPulvrizd*120¾ PrincSlvic120hd	Rail,dueled,driving	9
3Sep01-5Tim	fst	4f	:221 :452	Md Sp Wt 21k	33	10	3	47		58½	511½	Klinger C O	L 120	3.30	86-06	*Cool Cash*1152¾ *Ameri Brilliance*1133½ *Inner Command*120½	No factor, rail	10

WORKS: Oct18 Lrl 5f gd 1:04 B *8/8* Sep29 Lrl 4f fst :49 B *8/28* ●Aug18 Lrl 4f fst :483 H *1/8* ●Aug6 Lrl 4f fst :48 B *1/17*
TRAINER: Dirt(51 .08 $1.27) Sprint(33 .09 $1.59) Claim(32 .06 $1.13)

The example of Right Too Refuse covers all the bases for a bounce:

4 Right Too Refuse
Own: Young Chris
Dark Blue, White Hoop, White Hoops — $35,000
GRYDER A T (65 10 6 8 .15) 2002:(882 98 .11)

Dk. b or br c. 3 (Mar)
Sire: Lost Code (Codex) $7,500
Dam: Not Too Proper(Proper Reality)
Br: Chris Young & Elizabeth A DiBella (Ky)
Tr: Hushion Michael E(20 7 1 4 .35) 2002:(179 32 .18)

L 119

Life	10	1	1	2	$44,125	87
2002	6	0	1	1	$14,845	87
2001	4	1	0	1	$29,280	65
Aqu	3	0	1	0	$8,140	87
D.Fst	9	1	1	1	$40,660	87
Wet(350)	1	0	0	1	$3,465	67
Turf(300)	0	0	0	0	$0	–
Dst(330)	3	0	1	0	$9,430	87

Previously trained by Perry William W

8Nov02-5Aqu	fst	1	:231 :452 1:092 1:361 3↑	Alw 48000N2L	69	3	31	44	53½	65¾	59	Bridgmohan S X	L 117 fb	9.70	76-20	Phish1171¼ D' Coach1171¾ Make My Millenium1143	Posed no threat	7
27Oct02-2Aqu	fst	1	:233 :454 1:094 1:351	Clm 40000(40-30)	87	5	32	32½	21	2½	2hd	Prado E S	L 119 fb	5.50	90-12	FnAndDnd119hd RghtTRfs1193¾ ***Stnnthdcthb***1193¾	Battled gamely outside	6
11Oct02-9Bel	sly	7f	:223 :46 1:112 1:243	Clm 35000(35-30)	67	4	2	89¾	88¾	49½	36	Bermudez J E	L 119 f	13.80	74-25	Showtm1181 PruvnSummr1195 RghtTooRfs119nk	Very wide throughout	8
30Sep02-7Del	fst	1	:232 :464 1:123 1:382	Alw 43600N1x	35	5	1hd	2½	56	513	529¼	Black A S	L 117 b	5.00	61-19	Mt. Moran1174¾ Pop A Top Again1176 Plain Clothes1194	Used up	7
6Sep02-5Med	fst	170	:214 :444 1:093 1:391 3↑	Alw 30000N1x	59	1	31½	41	62½	79	614½	Beckner D V	L 114 b	*1.90	84-11	Excited1165¾ O'malley114nk Street Life1144	Chased, faded	7
11Aug02-6Mth	fst	6f	:211 :44 :562 1:092	Alw 33000N2L	69	6	1	43½	43½	44¼	48½	Ferrer J C	L 122 b	14.60	83-11	Moe's Mon117¾ *Wild Pro*1222½ *Threat OfVictory*1175¼	Wide turn,lugged in	7
24Nov01-7Aqu	fst	1⅛	:481 1:13 1:383 1:511	Remsen-G2	62	4	32	4¾	62¼	79½	715¼	Velez J A Jr	L 116 b	68.50	65-16	Saarland116nk Nokoma1163 Silent Fred1162¼	Steadied first turn	9
27Oct01-3Med	fst	170	:221 :462 1:13 1:433	Md Sp Wt 44k	65	1	43	1hd	1½	14½	14½	Velez J A Jr	L 118 b	2.40	76-17	RghtTooRfs1184½ AgstSng1187 TstyChrdngh1183¾	Steadied twice,in hand	9
18Oct01-5Med	fst	6f	:22 :45 :573 1:11	Md 50000(50-45)	61	1	8	54¾	55	55¾	31	Velez J A Jr	L 118 b	4.30	83-16	Stormy Day1181 Noles113hd *Right TooRefuse*1183½	Angled out,closed well	11
3Oct01-5Med	fst	5½f	:212 :442 :56 1:022	Md Sp Wt 38k	53	5	9	912	915	810	615	Velez J A Jr	118	8.30	94-10	Onthedeanslist1181 *Max's Buddy*1184½ Drawn Sword1136½	No factor	10

WORKS: Nov21 Bel tr.t 3f fst :364 B *4/27* Oct21 Mth 5f fst 1:02 B *3/4* Sep29 Mth 3f fst :38 B *14/20* Sep20 Mth 5f fst 1:015 B *9/24* Aug31 Mth 5f fst 1:013 H *2/23*
TRAINER: 1stW/Tm(26 .12 $0.58) Dirt(303 .19 $1.64) Claim(85 .16 $1.65)

A more subdued, more common example is Wind Knot:

3 Wind Knot
Own: Lewis James F
Blue, White Sash & Lf, Blue & White — $15,000
FOGELSONGER R (236 59 33 42 .25) 2002:(1028 223 .22)

B. f. 3 (Apr) EASDEC99 $7,500
Sire: Not For Love (Mr. Prospector) $15,000
Dam: Anytime Anyway(Tunerup)
Br: Dave & Leslie Krohn (Pa)
Tr: Barr Donald H(13 3 3 1 .23) 2002:(130 15 .12)

L 116 5

Life	5	1	2	2	$19,140	52
2002	5	1	2	2	$19,140	52
2001	0	M	0	0	$0	–
Lrl	3	1	2	0	$14,850	52
D.Fst	4	1	2	1	$16,830	52
Wet(420)	1	0	0	1	$2,310	33
Turf(285)	0	0	0	0	$0	–
Dst(330)	1	1	0	0	$8,550	42

25Oct02-3Lrl	fst	7f	:233 :473 1:141 1:281 3↑	ⒻMd 25000(25-20)	42	5	1	1hd	11½	11½	12	Fogelsonger R5	L 116 f	*.70	66-22	Wind Knot1162 True Facts1211¼ Dimpled121hd	Drifted 4wd 1/4,drivng	9
9Oct02-4Lrl	fst	6f	:224 :464 :591 1:12 3↑	ⒻMd 25000(25-20)	52	7	5	32½	3½	1hd	2nk	Alvarado F T	L 121 f	2.90	79-19	Polish Valentine116nk *Wind Knot*1215¼ Deceptive1213½	3wd,dueled,gamely	8
5Sep02-1Pim	fst	6f	:234 :472 1:001 1:133 3↑	ⒻMd 40000(40-35)	47	5	6	55¼	46	45½	34½	Alvarado F T	L 120 f	3.40	72-20	Roman In The Hills120½ Laser Cat1204 Wind Knot120½	Drifted wide 1/4	7
24Aug02-1Tim	my	*6½f	:232 :48 1:161 1:214 3↑	ⒻMd Sp Wt 21k	33	6	6	54	31½	31½	32¼	Goodwin N	L 119 f	*1.10	70-28	*PerfectBusinss*1191¾ LdyDiscrt119½ WindKnot119½	Wide turns, flattened	6
15Aug02-8Lrl	fst	6f	:23 :463 :591 1:121 3↑	ⒻMd 25000(25-20)	52	4	8	2hd	1hd	2hd	21	Goodwin N	L 119 f	15.20	77-22	Mara Queen1141 Wind Knot1193½ Strike Free1192½	Sluggish start,game	8

WORKS: Oct4 Lrl 5f fst 1:023 B *16/20* Sep20 Lrl 4f fst :51 Hg *24/28*
TRAINER: Dirt(277 .11 $1.42) Sprint(223 .12 $1.45) Claim(131 .10 $1.78)

The irony here, of course, is that Wind Knot bounced pretty severely from his draining, all-out second on October 9. But his 10-point-lower Beyer was still enough to win by two lengths.

This leads us to that troublesome offshoot of bounce theory: the "bounce and win," a further annoying complication in the whole subject. As we said earlier with top-figure horses, you often have to judge not only whether that horse will run a lower Beyer Speed Figure, but also whether he will decline enough to enable the rest of the field to bridge the Beyer gap. That was the problem handicappers faced in the 2002 Woodward Stakes at Belmont Park on September 7. Lido Palace, the 1-5 favorite, had an enormous edge on all his rivals—a minimum of 12 points, and in most cases more than 20 points.

8 Lido Palace (Chi)
Own:Amerman Racing Stables
Dark Blue, White Epaulets, White Hoops
CHAVEZ J F (67 9 6 7 .13) 2002:(941 177 .19)

Ch. h. 5
Sire: Rich Man's Gold (Forty Niner) $3,954
Dam:Sonada*Chi(Quick Decision)
Br: Haras Figuron (Chi)
Tr: Frankel Robert(14 4 2 3 .29) 2002:(361 88 .24)

L 126

Life	20	9	6	2	$2,188,574	119	D.Fst	18	8	5	2	$2,152,494	119
2002	4	1	1	1	$497,500	119	Wet(316)	1	1	0	0	$18,630	–
2001	6	2	2	1	$1,240,000	116	Turf(224)	1	0	1	0	$17,450	–
Bel	4	2	2	0	$800,000	116	Dst(243)	4	1	3	0	$335,580	116

7Sep02-9Bel	fst	1⅛	:454 1:093 1:344 1:473	3↑ Woodward-G1	105	1	31½	31½	42	3½	1¾	Chavez J F	L 126 b	*.45	92–06	Lido Palace126¾ Gander126nk Express Tour1267¾	Came wide, driving	6
3Aug02-9Sar	fst	1⅛	:454 1:091 1:34 1:47	3↑ Whitney H-G1	119	4	410	39	47½	33	31¼	Chavez J F	L 119 b	3.80	103–07	Left Bank1181¼ Street Cry123no *Lido Palace*1191½	Game finish outside	6
6Jly02-10Bel	fst	1¼	:483 1:124 1:37 2:004	3↑ Suburban H-G2	113	3	33½	31½	21	21½	2¾	Bailey J D	L 119 b	2.65	89–10	E Dubai116¾ Lido Palace1191 Macho Uno1193¾	3 wide, game finish	7
3Feb02-6SA	fst	1⅛	:473 1:113 1:361 1:483	4↑ SanAntonioH-G2	103	4	52½	42	42	42¾	43	Bailey J D	LB 121 b	*.80	90–17	Redattore116½ Euchre1191½ Irisheyesareflying1171	Stalked btwn,no bid	7
24Nov01♦Tokyo(Jpn)	fst	*1 5/16	LH 2:054	3↑ Japan Cup Dirt-G1							813½	Bailey J D	126 b	2.50		Kurofune1217 Wing Arrow126½ Miracle Opera126¾		16
Timeform rating: 108				Stk 2055000												*Wide in 7th,5th 2-1/2f out,weakened 1-1/2f out.Generous Rosi 9th*		
8Sep01-9Bel	fst	1⅛	:463 1:101 1:343 1:472	3↑ Woodward-G1	113	3	31	31	3½	2½	11	Bailey J D	L 126 b	2.90	93–14	Lido Palace1261 Albert TheGreat126½ Tiznow1268¼	Determinedly outside	5
28Jly01-6Sar	fst	1⅛	:463 1:101 1:344 1:474	3↑ Whitney H-G1	114	3	53	53	42	1½	12	Bailey J D	L 115 b	2.95	102 —	*Lido Palace*1152 Albert The Great124nk Gander113nk	4 wide move, driving	7
1Jly01-8Bel	fst	1¼	:463 1:102 1:35 2:001	3↑ Suburban H-G2	116	5	31½	31	21½	21½	22¼	Flores D R	L 115 b	4.10	91–07	Albert The Great1232¼ *Lido Palace*115hd Include1227	Inside run, gamely	6
19May01-7Haw	fst	1¼	:461 1:101 1:354 2:013	3↑ HawGoldCupH-G2	114	3	53	45	32	23	21¼	Flores D R	L 114	3.40	96–23	Duckhorn1121¼ Lido Palace1147½ *Guided Tour*116nk	Gaining late	7
24Mar01♦NadAlSheba(UAE)	fst	*1⅛	LH 1:47	UAE Derby-G3							36	Bailey J D	128	-		Express Tour122hd Street Cry1226 Lido Palace1283½		14
Timeform rating: 109				Stk 2000000												*Rated in 5th,3rd 2f out,no further response.Tapatio 6th*		

WORKS: **Sep26 Bel 3f fst :373 B** *7/12* **Sep19 Bel 4f fst :492 B** *19/43* **Sep1 Sar tr.t 4f fst :503 B** *5/15* **Aug26 Sar 5f fst 1:004 B** *10/31* **Aug18 Sar 4f fst :484 B** *8/49* **Aug1 Sar 3f fst :352 B** *2/12*
TRAINER: Dirt(204 .27 $1.87) Routes(590 .26 $1.81) GrdStk(259 .27 $1.96)

But Lido Palace was coming off a huge effort in the Whitney, where he had earned a lifetime-best 119, and you could very well anticipate some sort of bounce. But how bad? And could anyone improve enough to catch up with him? In the Woodward, Lido Palace did indeed bounce badly, all the way down to a 105. He struggled every step, only managing to survive by three-quarters of a length. He bounced badly, and yet he still won.

This is not an infrequent occurrence. Take the example of Nevada Kid:

Nevada Kid
Own: Delfiner Marvin & Fink Morton

Ch. c. 3 (Feb) FTFFEB01 $250,000
Sire: Carson City (Mr. Prospector) $35,000
Dam: In the District(Kris S.)
Br: C Peter Beler (Ky)
Tr: Matz Michael R (—) 2002:(236 36 .15)

Life	3	2	0	0	$51,900	96	D.Fst	3	2	0	0	$51,900	96
2002	3	2	0	0	$51,900	96	Wet(420)	0	0	0	0	$0	–
2001	0	M	0	0	$0	–	Turf(290)	0	0	0	0	$0	–
CSC	0	0	0	0	$0	–	Dist	0	0	0	0	$0	–

28Oct02-7Del	fst	1	:24 :474 1:131 1:402	Alw 43600N1X	79	6	21½	22½	2hd	11	11	McCarthy M J	L 122 f	*.60	80–22	Nevada Kid1221 Starlit Marque1171 Hilty117nk	Roused to hold sway	7
2Oct02-1Del	fst	1 1/16	:234 :474 1:12 1:434	3↑ Md Sp Wt 39k	96	1	11½	1½	12½	15	14½	McCarthy M J	L 120 f	3.80	89–14	*Nevada Kid*1204½ Addicks12016 Personal Clearance1201	Much the best	6
12Sep02-6Bel	fst	7f	:23 :47 1:133 1:27	3↑ Md Sp Wt 45k	64	4	8	77	77½	59½	47¾	Bailey J D	120 f	5.90	60–28	*Abduction*123½ Survivor Kippy1205¾ Tarakan1201½	3 wide trip, no rally	8

As in the case of Lido Palace, Nevada Kid held a seemingly insurmountable advantage over his opposition—anywhere from 16 to 30 points. But you had to try to beat him. After all, he had just won his maiden, with first-time Lasix, with a clear lead, and now had the potential for a big bounce. And bounce he did, all the way to a 79. In the end, however, after an exhausting stretch battle, he still won by a length.

The example of Senor Mac is worth a long look. It illustrates many of the complicating elements, as well as the logic of making judgments about bounces.

12 Senor Mac
Own:MacMillen William C Jr
Light Green/dark Green Hoops, Dark
LUZZI M J (20 3 2 0 .15) 2002:(1000 110 .11)

B. g. 3 (May) EASMAY01 $60,000
Sire: Distinctive Pro (Mr. Prospector) $10,000
Dam: Topper B. Bold(Bold L. B.)
Br: Donald E Jacobs & Patricia A Jacobs (NY)
Tr: Gyarmati Leah(3 0 0 1 .00) 2002:(166 14 .08)

L 121

Life	7	M	2	0	$21,320	70	
2002	6	M	2	0	$18,860	70	
2001	1	M	0	0	$2,460	58	
Aqu ⊡	0	0	0	0	$0	–	
D.Fst	6	0	1	0	$13,120	70	
Wet(340)	1	0	1	0	$8,200	69	
Turf(245)	0	0	0	0	$0	–	
Dst(345)	1	0	0	0	$0	24	

Previously trained by Bond Harold James

2Nov02- 1Aqu	fst	1	$:23^2$ $:46^4$ $1:11^4$ $1:38^1$	3↑	[S]Md Sp Wt 44k	35	10	$3^{1\frac12}$	$4^{1\frac34}$	$5^{6\frac12}$	7^{14}	$9^{19\frac12}$	Prado E S	L 120 fb	5.60	55–22	NothingWsted120^1 IndinCrd$120^{4\frac12}$ WhiskyChsr115^{nk}	Stumbled start, wide	11
29Sep02-10Bel	fst	1	$:23^2$ $:46^4$ $1:12^3$ $1:39^4$	3↑	[S]Md Sp Wt 44k	19	2	$1^{\frac12}$	$2^{\frac12}$	3^2	11^{13}	$12^{27\frac12}$	Prado E S	L 118 b	*3.00	42–26	BlckAndBls$118^{1\frac12}$ KngOfThMont$118^{1\frac14}$ JllyRllRck$122^{\frac34}$	Dueled inside, tired	12
30Aug02- 9Sar	gd	7f	$:22^3$ $:46^1$ $1:12^1$ $1:26^1$	3↑	[S]Md Sp Wt 41k	69	3	9	$6^{3\frac34}$	$4^{1\frac34}$	2^2	$2^{2\frac14}$	Prado E S	L 119 b	*1.90	72–21	Indoughrty'shonor$119^{2\frac14}$ SnorMc$119^{\frac34}$ OtkJustPrinc$114^{1\frac12}$	3 wide, got place	10
12Aug02- 9Sar	fst	7f	$:22^4$ $:46^2$ $1:12$ $1:25^4$	3↑	[S]Md Sp Wt 41k	70	3	7	2^{hd}	1^{hd}	2^{hd}	2^{nk}	Prado E S	L 118 b	4.90	76–20	BagsArePacked118^{nk} SenorMac$118^{3\frac14}$ GrnSsso$118^{3\frac14}$	Stumbled start, inside	10
14Jly02- 1Bel	fst	7f	$:22^4$ $:46^3$ $1:11^3$ $1:24^1$	3↑	[S]Md Sp Wt 41k	51	5	8	$9^{4\frac12}$	$7^{2\frac34}$	4^6	4^{12}	Prado E S	L 118 b	7.50	70–17	SmokAndFm$118^{5\frac12}$ JllyRollRock$123^{4\frac12}$ BgsArPckd118^2	Inside trip, no rally	14
22Jun02- 1Bel	fst	6f	$:22^4$ $:46^1$ $:58^1$ $1:10^1$	3↑	[S]Md Sp Wt 41k	24	11	9	$9^{1\frac34}$	$11^{9\frac34}$	10^{23}	11^{26}	Prado E S	L 117 fb	3.00	61–10	One NThree117^{12} Ben'sGoodDeed$117^{\frac34}$ [D]StormCity117^{nk}	7 wide trip, tired	12
2Sep01- 3Sar	fst	6½f	$:23$ $:46^4$ $1:11^4$ $1:18^2$		[S]Md Sp Wt 41k	58	7	6	$8^{3\frac12}$	4^1	$4^{2\frac12}$	4^5	Prado E S	L 118 b	3.65	78–14	NvrGivIn118^{nk} LostInThWoods118^{hd} BrssTngo$118^{4\frac12}$	Awkward start, 4 wide	10

WORKS: Dec8 Bel tr.t 3f fst :36 B *2/19* Dec2 Bel tr.t 4f fst $:49^2$ B *5/44* Oct28 Bel 5f fst 1:02 B *28/38* Oct21 Bel 5f fst 1:02 B *23/43* Oct15 Bel tr.t 4f fst $:49^1$ B *36/188* Sep24 Bel tr.t 4f fst $:49^4$ B *7/17*
TRAINER: 1stW/Tm(41 .10 $0.82) Route/Sprint(33 .06 $2.16) 31-60Days(64 .13 $1.40) Dirt(313 .09 $1.63) Sprint(194 .08 $1.61) MdnSpWt(45 .16 $4.01)

The brief career of Senor Mac illustrates some of the vagaries of anticipating a bounce. He was a clear case of three-and-out, and his race on August 12 had the classic pattern of overexertion—dueling the entire trip and losing by only a neck at seven furlongs. So, on August 30, as the 9-5 favorite, you had to bet against him. Unfortunately, while he didn't win that race, he still ran very well—earning virtually the same Beyer as he had nearly three weeks earlier. As with many younger, more lightly raced horses, he didn't bounce the way you would expect him to. But on September 29 he looked even more vulnerable. Now he had run back-to-back big Beyers, and he was much more likely to bounce. In that race, after dueling for the lead at a mile, he collapsed completely, and his Beyer plummeted to a 19.

Pretty Wild presents a somewhat similar case—though at a much higher level. When he was entered in the Champagne Stakes at Belmont Park on October 5 he was bet very heavily.

Pretty Wild			
Own: Robsham Einar P			

B. c. 2 (Mar)
Sire: Wild Again (Icecapade) $50,000
Dam: Pretty Discreet(Private Account)
Br: E Paul Robsham (Ky)
Tr: Hough Stanley M (—) 2002:(215 38 .18)

	Life	6 1 2 2	$145,260	99
	2002	6 1 2 2	$145,260	99
	2001	0 M 0 0	$0	–
	CSC	0 0 0 0	$0	–

D.Fst	5 1 1 2	$105,260	99
Wet(365)	1 0 1 0	$40,000	99
Turf(295)	0 0 0 0	$0	–
Dist	0 0 0 0	$0	–

5Oct02–9Bel fst 1¹⁄₁₆ :231 :47 1:12 1:442 Champagne-G1 85 9 63½ 63½ 51½ 45½ 47 Bridgmohan S X L122 *1.30 71–22 Toccet122½ Icecoldbertrds122³ Erinsouthrnmn122¾ 4 wide move, faded 9
15Sep02–9Bel gd 1 :222 :452 1:101 1:361 Futurity-G1 99 5 53 51½ 3½ 2³ 21½ Bridgmohan S X L120 3.75 86–22 Whywhywhy120¹½ PrettyWild120⁵½ TruckleFtur120⁶½ Game finish outside 7
31Aug02–8Sar fst 7f :222 :453 1:102 1:23 Hopeful-G1 99 2 6 2½ 2¹ 1½ 21¾ Bridgmohan S X L122 17.30 88–13 Sky Mesa122¹¾ Pretty Wild122² Zavata122⁵½ Bid 1/4pl, 2nd best 6
13Jly02–3Bel fst 6f :221 :454 :583 1:11 Md Sp Wt 43k 81 4 6 4² 52½ 1hd 15 Bridgmohan S X L119 5.90 83–20 Pretty Wild119⁵ Blakelock119²½ Midnight Charlie119nk Stumbled start 9
9Jun02–3Bel fst 5½f :23 :461 :59 1:06 Md Sp Wt 43k 54 2 1 2½ 3½ 3⁶ 3⁴ Davis R G L117 4.20 78–17 Desert Warrior117hd Stroll117⁵¾ Pretty Wild117hd Vied inside, weakened 7
27May02–3Bel fst 5f :223 :453 :57³ Md Sp Wt 43k 59 2 4 54½ 55 48½ 39¾ Davis R G L117 18.10 85–13 Zavata117⁵½ Lion Tamer117⁴½ Pretty Wild117¾ Greenly inside 6

Once again you have a very young, lightly raced horse who ran a huge 99 after a brief layoff. With a horse of this type it is hard to make a definitive judgment about any bounce. He is a classy, extremely well-bred runner with unlimited potential, and he had run a very powerful effort on July 13. So on August 31 you had to wait and see. But, when Pretty Wild ran another 99, you now had a pattern that had to be seen as a strong bounce possibility. In the Champagne, Pretty Wild did not run badly, but he did regress to a Beyer of only 85.

The examples of Senor Mac and Pretty Wild remind us that, as with every other handicapping approach, judgments have to be made in every situation where you might detect a potential bounce. In some cases those judgments will not be sustained in the running. Such occasional disappointments cannot be avoided in this game. But, despite these setbacks, the process of looking for horses with the characteristics of a bounce should be part of every player's approach, and this approach should be an absolutely essential part of any strategy that uses the Beyer Speed Figures. If you can identify a favorite who will bounce badly—and the great majority of these peak performers are heavily bet—you could be working on a big score.

A clear-cut illustration of this came in the sixth race at Calder Race Course on October 17. The potential bouncer was Erin of Wicklow. She had shown a consistent pattern over her last eight races. Back in June, after she jumped up from a 51 to a 68, she regressed to a 39, and then improved again to a 44 and a 67 in her last start before the October 17 race. So, in the two most recent instances when she moved up to a figure in the mid-to-upper 60's, she couldn't sustain that level. Of course, there was no guarantee that she would repeat the same pattern over again, but her recent history strongly suggested that possibility. And if she did bounce once again, at odds of 3-2, that would break the race wide open.

In this nine-horse field you could make a logical case for only three other horses. This trio consistently ran Beyers in the mid-to-upper 50's. The remaining five runners simply did not match up in terms of figures. These three contenders finished 1-2-3 at odds of 9-2, 5-1, and 2-1. The exacta paid $68.40 and the triple paid $204.60. While there was some luck involved (Erin of Wicklow broke slowly and closed mildly to finish fourth), the lesson is clear: Take aim against these potential bouncers and you open up the race to big value. You will not be right every time, but when you are, the price will be substantial. And, in the long run, that makes all the difference.

Finding flaws in big-Beyer horses is often the key to finding value. The seventh race at Calder on October 19 provides another clear example. In this eight-horse field of $5,000 claimers, there were two horses who simply did not figure at all. Of the remaining six horses, two of them had strong indications of a bounce:

- Great Baron. Before his last race he had run Beyers of 47-56-57-43-42. Then he dropped to $5,000 and suddenly jumped up to a lifetime-best 72—a huge increase of around 30 points from his two previous races. That dramatic, out-of-nowhere leap in Beyer figures is a clear warning sign that a severe negative reaction could be coming. He was 5-1. His Beyer fell to 43.
- Te Deum. This colt had frequent gaps in his form, a sure indication of physical problems. He had been dropped to $10,000 claiming on July 12 and ran up the track. After

another $2^{1}/_{2}$-month layoff he was all out to win by a half-length, earning a lifetime-best Beyer of 77. The comment line said, "Bore out badly stretch." His trainer now was dropping him again to $5,000. All the indications were negative. Te Deum went off at 5-2. His Beyer fell to 55.

The Beyer figures of the remaining four horses were impossible to separate. But they all had one thing in common: They consistently ran figures in the mid-to-upper 60's. A four-horse exacta and trifecta box made perfect sense. The potential bouncers, Te Deum and Great Baron, ran out, and three of the four remaining contenders finished 1-2-3. The trifecta paid $302.40.

Of course, not every race breaks down so neatly. Nor does every Te Deum and Great Baron bounce according to plan, or bounce badly enough to finish completely out of the money. But finding weaknesses in such seemingly "logical" horses—counterpunching, if you will—should be a principal weapon in your arsenal. Targeting bouncing favorites and other overbet runners is one of the most profitable uses of the Beyer figures.

Unfortunately, it's really not possible to do any kind of reliable macrostatistical study on bouncers. The problems with definitions are simply overwhelming. We can, however, extrapolate some useful insights from other studies that flirt around the edges of bounce theory. For example, the three-and-out study in *Beyer On Speed* gives some indication of what happens to the Beyer figures of most horses after they improve to higher levels. Perhaps even more valuable is an analysis of horses who just ran lifetime-best Beyers. This offers a more manageable way to investigate this important topic.

Before making such a study, some sensible ground rules had to be applied:

1. Since young horses or horses with very few starts are constantly establishing new lifetime bests and can have notoriously erratic form, only horses with more than 10 starts were

considered. The idea of a lifetime best is only meaningful when a horse first establishes some sort of maturity and stability in his form.

2. Only dirt form was used. If a horse ran on the turf immediately after a lifetime-best figure, that horse was not included.

3. If a long layoff (more than three months) intervened after a lifetime best, that horse also was not considered.

Under these ground rules, here are the results for a sample of 1,000 horses that had just run a lifetime-best Beyer: The next time out, 87.9 percent ran a lower figure, while 12.1 percent ran the same Beyer figure or a higher figure in their next start. Most startlingly, only one horse in a thousand improved by more than nine points after running a lifetime best.

Here's a further breakdown:

- 7.9 percent declined by 30 points or more in their next start.
- 13.4 percent declined between 20 and 29 points.
- 31.8 percent declined between 10 and 19 points.

So, more than half of the lifetime-besters declined by 10 points or more, a drop of between 10 and 19 points being most frequent.

These are dramatic results, or so it would appear. But statistics are funny things. If you turn them just a bit and look at them from a different angle, they might say something quite different. For example, if you create a category called Virtually Unchanged—that is, horses whose Beyers declined or improved by only three points either way—that category would include 18.5 percent of the runners. And if you add in the 3.7 percent who improved by four points or more, you now have 22.2 percent performing quite strongly after running a lifetime-best figure. That's a somewhat less startling result than the 12.1 percent who had repeated their lifetime best or improved upon it.

In a final category, 24.5 percent of the thousand horses declined by between four and nine points. Since these horses, by definition, were all coming off peak efforts, a single-digit drop in their Beyers could very well mean that they would still be significant factors in their next starts. In other words, even if you expected a slight regression from their new lifetime bests, that did *not* necessarily mean that you could dismiss these horses next time they ran. A decline of five or six or seven points could still leave these horses very much in the mix.

Clearly, the dramatic results of this study should not lead to any mindless, wholesale dismissal of all lifetime-best runners in their next starts. Still, some useful conclusions can safely be made:

1. When a horse returns after a lifetime-best Beyer, you should treat that horse with considerable skepticism. Nearly 80 percent will run substantially worse next time, and, while one in five of these runners will perform reasonably well in their next race, the generally low price of these runners will most often not be worth the risk anyway.

2. Most of the horses who continued to improve their Beyers after an initial lifetime best did so between their 11th and their 15th starts. When a horse has had more than 15 starts in his career, the chances of improving after a lifetime best decline significantly.

3. Horses who achieve a lifetime best on a wet track are particularly vulnerable next time out. Special circumstances—such as a wire-to-wire win on a sloppy track—can often lead to a peak performance. When you take away those special circumstances, everything changes.

4. For the subset of horses that jumped up more than 20 points from their previous races to reach a new lifetime best, there was a slight shift in the percentages. For example, 7.9 percent of all lifetime bests reacted by running 30 or more points lower next time out. But among horses that jumped up 20 or

more points to reach that new top, 11.3 percent ran 30 or more points lower—a slight increase. And that tendency holds for every other category. While, among all lifetime bests, 53.1 percent declined by 10 or more points, that percentage increased to 67.1 percent among the more limited group. The percentage that improved their figures by four or more points decreased from 3.7 percent for the entire sample down to 2.0 percent for the smaller group. So, the greater the leap up to a lifetime best, the greater the chance of a reaction the next time out.

LIFETIME-BEST PERCENTAGES

BEYER FIGURE AFTER LIFETIME BEST	TOTAL SAMPLE	HORSES IMPROVING BY 20 PTS. OR MORE BEFORE LIFETIME BEST
30 or more	7.9 %	11.3 %
20 to -29	13.4 %	18.0 %
10 to -19	31.8 %	32.4 %
4 to -9	24.5 %	21.1 %
3 to +3	18.5 %	15.2 %
+4 and up	3.7 %	2.0 %

Of course, no assumption or theory or statistical study in handicapping is without its many exceptions. In particular, you have to be aware of how an unusually successful trainer can consistently defy the probabilities that apply to more ordinary conditioners.

Take the case of Ozilda's Karen. She was a decent enough filly, running occasional figures into the 70's at tracks such as Great Lakes Downs and later Tampa Bay Downs. Early in her 4-year-old season she had run impressively at Tampa, winning by five lengths in a $25,000 claimer and earning a lifetime-best Beyer of 78. Then she put in a series of decent efforts over her next six races, but couldn't again reach that 78 Beyer.

On June 19, however, after 26 trips around the track, her life suddenly changed. She was claimed by trainer Scott Lake. One month later she finished second for $50,000 with a Beyer of 79. That was marginally a new lifetime best. Two weeks later she won by 5¾ lengths. Her Beyer catapulted to 95. That was a more spectacular lifetime best. One month later she won by seven lengths. Her Beyer improved again to a 98—yet another lifetime best. In a multitude of ways, the experience of Ozilda's Karen defied the statistical probabilities.

But handicappers are no longer surprised by such exceptional performances when they come from a certain select group of high-percentage barns. And they know that statistical studies, while they can be strongly suggestive, should never be considered decisive in any specific race—especially in the very special circumstances when trainers such as Scott Lake step in to transform the careers of formerly ordinary racehorses.

A more common example of the limits of statistical studies is symbolized by the 5-year-old gelding Whitewaterspritzer. In the ninth race at Belmont on October 2, 2002, he had the top Beyer figure of 98—a new lifetime best for him. A repeat of that effort would surely win this $45,000 claimer. Even a slight decline would make him very tough to beat. The speed figure of Whitewaterspritzer did indeed decline somewhat, down to a 92. And this six-point drop in his figures would swell the mass of data showing how the great majority of horses running lifetime bests don't run as well next time out. But he still won by 1¾ lengths, proving that lifetime bests can also bounce and win. And he paid $6. All of which confirms once again how complicated this subject can be, and how carefully you must weigh the prospects of a bounce when you are constructing any wager.

The conclusion, however, remains compelling: A dynamic approach to the Beyer figures—projecting change, in this case decline, especially among shorter-priced horses—is often the key to value. And without value, we horseplayers perish.

4

BEYER PATTERNS AND CYCLES

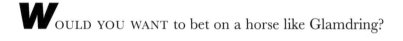

WOULD YOU WANT to bet on a horse like Glamdring?

7 Glamdring
Own:Leo Villareal
Yellow, Charcoal Gray Ball, Gray Sleeves
ARROYO N JR (75 11 7 7 .15) 2002:(749 95 .13)

Dk. b or br g. 3 (May)
Sire: Marquetry (Conquistador Cielo) $15,000
Dam: Zacatecana (Slew o' Gold)
Br: Butterfield Interest Inc (Ky)
Tr: Tesher Howard M(7 1 1 1 .14) 2002:(114 5 .04)

L 121

Life	9	2	2	1	$70,430	97	D.Fst	6	1	1	1	$45,730	97
2002	8	1	2	1	$54,530	97	Wet(295)	2	1	0	0	$15,900	67
2001	1	1	0	0	$15,900	64	Turf(280)	1	0	1	0	$8,800	87
Aqu	2	1	1	0	$35,600	97	Dst(325)	5	2	0	1	$53,030	97

27Sep02-7Bel	my	7f		:214	:441	1:093	1:223	3↑ Alw 47000N2L	67	3	7	3½	3½	49	713	Bailey J D	L118	11.10	77-13	*Onthedeanslist*1184 D' Coach1186½ Our Song120nk	Chased 3 wide, tired	10
7Sep02-6Bel	fst	7f		:222	:453	1:102	1:233	3↑ Alw 47000N1X	59	6	4	72½	51¼	613	612¾	Bridgmohan S X	L118	5.90	72-13	Fire Blitz118nk Drifting Song1181¼ Unbridled Trick1181¾	4 wide trip, tired	9
10Aug02-8Sar	fst	6f		:22	:452	:572	1:101	3↑ Alw 47000N2L	85	2	8	919	87½	68¾	49½	Arroyo N Jr	L117	36.25	81-11	Warners1178 Unbridled Dignity1211¼ *Fire Blitz*114nk	Bumped start, rallied	9
12Apr02-8Aqu	fm	1 1/16	Ⓣ	:223	:473	1:114	1:434	3↑ Alw 44000N1X	87	1	34	42	31	11	22	Castellano J J	L114	4.80	83-15	Robbie'sRockin1112 Glmdring1143¼ PreferredGust119¾	Close up, gamely	10
22Mar02-7Aqu	fst	7f		:224	:454	1:111	1:24	Alw 43000N1X	81	7	2	66¾	65¼	32½	2nk	Pimentel J	L117	7.90	80-20	*It'sAMonster*119nk Glamdring1172¾ DynmicLord1171¾	Game finish outside	7
2Feb02-6Aqu	fst	6f	⊡	:231	:47	:59	1:114	Alw 43000N1X	72	2	2	45	44	39	35½	Pimentel J	L117	3.25	79-16	DoubleMyProspect1192 **FvoritSwp**1173½ Glmdring1172¼	Inside, no threat	5
3Jan02-8Aqu	fst	6f	⊡	:23	:464	:591	1:121	Alw 43000N1X	82	2	6	68	42½	41¼	2nk	Pimentel J	L119	28.25	83-21	C'sJckpot117nk [D]Glmdring119nk *DoublMyProspct*1223¼	Steadied, bumped	6
Disqualified and placed 4th																						
9Dec01-2Aqu	my	6f	⊡	:232	:471	:593	1:12	Md 60000 (60-50)	64	7	4	85½	42	1½	1½	Pimentel J5	116	25.75	85-14	Glamdring116½ *MyManRyn*1213 Prospect'sLegcy1211¼	Lugged in stretch	12

WORKS: **Nov10 Bel tr.t 4f fst :524 B** *68/70* **Oct15 Bel tr.t 4f fst :492 B** *51/188* **Aug28 Sar 5f fst 1:00 H** *2/26*
TRAINER: Dirt(193 .10 $1.67) Sprint(157 .08 $1.32) Alw(93 .06 $1.21)

If you paid careful attention to speed-figure patterns, you would take a horse like Glamdring very seriously indeed. You wouldn't dismiss him because of that ugly-looking recent form. Instead, you would see deeper into those past performances, and Glamdring would emerge as a horse with big potential and big value.

Finding the hidden Glamdrings of this world—that will be the focus of this chapter.

The search for patterns in the Beyer Speed Figures is based on a simple premise: What's important is not just the speed figure a horse earned in his *last* race, but how his recent Beyers led up to that figure. How does that figure fit into the overall pattern of Beyers for that horse? Can that pattern tell us anything valuable about what we can anticipate in that horse's next race?

If you want to get the most out of the Beyer Speed Figures, then, among other things, you need to look at the recent history and pattern of figures for each horse, and then fit that into the larger context of Beyer figures for all the other horses in that race. In many cases, taking this broader, more in-depth approach will reveal a great deal more than just looking at any single figure, even the most recent figure. And it will certainly create more value-oriented plays than would an overemphasis on the last-race Beyer. As we've already argued in analyzing top Beyers and bouncers, value often comes from projecting *decline* for shorter-priced horses. They become targets to bet against. But, just as often, value will come from predicting *improvement* for higher-priced horses. They become the focus for aggressive wagers. And speed-figure patterns can help uncover these plays.

Not surprisingly, the past performances of these fragile Thoroughbreds come in every conceivable shape, form, and outline. The number of possible configurations is, obviously, infinite. So it should also come as no surprise that the most frequently occurring pattern is . . . no pattern at all. With all the varied and changing circumstances that influence the racing life of any Thoroughbred—the myriad ailments and illnesses and operations, the changes in medications, track conditions, racetracks, trainers, classes, distances, surfaces, intervening layoffs, etc.—the speed figures of most racehorses cannot be expected to fall into any clearly discernible pattern.

These random runners represent the forces of disorder and chaos in Thoroughbred racing—that inscrutable patternless "form" we see in so many horses' past performances. When illogical, ridiculous-looking horses surprise us and win, we can be excused for thinking that disorder and chaos infect too much of the handicapper's world, and that we horseplayers are locked in a futile struggle to control these dark forces. In this struggle to bring some necessary order and sense to handicapping, speed-figure patterns can help. They represent the forces of order and predictability in a horse's past performances. When you can identify them and judge that they are relevant, you need to exploit that opportunity.

Fortunately, even if most horses don't fit neatly into any one category, there are a sufficient number whose past performances *do* form a pattern that it's worth identifying the principal types:

1. **Peak performers.** This is what the previous chapter on bouncers was all about—identifying those horses that might have overextended themselves in especially stressful and exhausting efforts. They are the potential bouncers.

2. **Repeat performers.** These horses show a remarkable consistency in their recent Beyers—a string of four or six or eight consecutive figures within a few points of one another (84-81-85-82-84-81). Of course, the string has to stop sometime, so there is no guarantee that a horse will repeat that same figure on any given day. And he certainly won't go on repeating that figure indefinitely into the future. In fact, unless there is a dramatic change in conditions, you can never really know when the streak will end. Still, these horses are generally more reliable. Although in most cases they have very limited upside potential, they can become solid bets if you can bounce higher-figure horses. As you might expect, an extended period of consistent figures most often occurs with higher-quality runners. Few cheaper horses can hold their form that long.

3. **Good fig/bad fig.** This is a rare species indeed, but there are periods in some Thoroughbreds' careers when they will alternate between a good race and a bad race. Mr. One Way is just such a remarkable case.

4 Mr. One Way
Own:Pre K Training Center
Hunter Green, Black Belt, Black Cuffs — $9,000
BLAKE J L (26 2 4 2 .08) 2002:(161 12 .07)

B. g. 3 (Mar) EASOCT00 $9,000
Sire: Secret Hello (Private Account) $2,500
Dam: Lustrous Sparkle(In Reality)
Br: Susan Shipp & Cynthia Bonnie (Va)
Tr: Deville Carl J(24 3 4 2 .13) 2002:(133 14 .11)

L 114

Life	22	3	2	3	$39,540	60	D.Fst	19	2	2	3	$32,850	60
2002	13	2	1	2	$18,030	58	Wet(275)	3	1	0	0	$6,690	55
2001	9	1	1	1	$21,510	60	Turf(255)	0	0	0	0	$0	–
Med	3	1	0	0	$9,880	59	Dst(320)	0	0	0	0	$0	–

7Oct02-4Pha	fst	5½f	:22^2 :47 :59^2 1:06^1	Clm 7500	51	5	7	8^{10}	8^{9¾}	8^{8½}	6^{5¼}	Blake J L	L 120 b	6.80	77-21	Stormin' Reprized120½ Snooze Zone120¾ Saratoga Bill120½	No factor	8
7Sep02-2Pha	fst	5½f	:22^1 :46^2 :59^1 1:06	Clm 7500	55	3	7	7^{9½}	7^{4½}	5^{3¼}	1^{nk}	Blake J L	L 120 b	9.70	83-19	Mr. One Way120^{nk} Snooze Zone120½ Nitro Express115^{2½}	Wide, just up	7
26Aug02-3Mth	fst	6f	:22^3 :45^4 :58^4 1:11^3	Clm 9000 (10-9)	40	1	5	1^{hd}	2½	4^{2½}	6^{11¾}	Blake J L	L 114 b	17.70	69-17	Shockittoem119^2 StrryIde119½ Mecke'sDncr116^{3½}	Vied inside,weakened	6
14Aug02-2Mth	fst	6f	:22^2 :45^4 :58^3 1:12^3	Clm 7500	52	1	8	8^{4½}	8^{7½}	7^{5½}	4^{2½}	Blake J L	L 119 b	3.60e	73-20	MyPortfolio116^{1½} DaButler116½ AleutinFrost116½	Slow early,steady gain	8
24Jly02-2Mth	gd	6f	:22^2 :46 :58^2 1:11^2	Clm 7500	37	7	9	8^3	7^{5¾}	9^{6½}	9^{10¾}	Blake J L	L 119 b	6.20e	71-17	*True Storm*116^4 Aleutian Frost116^{hd} *My Portfolio*119no	Wide, no rally	9
28Jun02-1Mth	gd	6f	:23 :46^4 :59^1 1:12^1	Clm 7500	55	1	6	1^{hd}	1½	1^{1½}	1^1	Staples C	L 116 b	7.20	78-19	Mr.OneWy116^1 DncingPretns116^1 Hydn'sLw116^4	Vied inside,clear,drvg	6
8Jun02-4Pha	fst	6f	:22^1 :46^2 :59^2 1:12^1	3↑ Clm 5000N2L	42	6	5	3^2	3^1	3^4	3^{7¾}	Santagata N	L 115 b	*1.70	70-19	Loverboy Rebel120^7 Mister Fancy113¾ *Mr.OneWay*115^{3¾}	Eased out, tired	7
21May02-4Del	fst	6f	:23 :47^1 1:00^1 1:13^3	Clm 8000 (8-7)	52	6	1	1½	2^{hd}	3^3	6^{4¾}	Martin E M Jr	L 116 b	10.50	70-25	MonstrMon119^{2¾} WootiToot116½ SuvNoblmn119^{nk}	Vied inside, weakened	7
27Apr02-10CD	sly	6½f	:23 :46^4 1:13 1:20	3↑ Clm 12500N2L	35	11	2	5^{2½}	6^{4¼}	12^{15}	12^{13¾}	Bramblett J	L 111 b	42.00	57-23	Knights Sovereign119^{nk} Acountforthecash119^{nk} Senor Will119½	Faded	12
12Apr02-5Spt	fst	6f	:22 :45^4 :58 1:11^1	Clm 12500N2L	37	7	5	5^{6½}	5^6	4^7	4^{9½}	Cadman Z	L 117 b	10.70	81-11	BlueEyedTiger117^{hd} JulesPride117^{4¼} MinnesotaPitch117^5	Broke outward	7

WORKS: ●Sep29 Mth 3f fst :35^4 B *1/20* Jly19 Mth 3f fst :36 B *3/13*
TRAINER: Sprint/Route(34 .03 $1.09) Dirt(318 .08 $1.44) Routes(57 .04 $0.98) Claim(113 .10 $1.69)

Once again, you can't just assume the pattern will continue indefinitely, but it can give you a lead to follow, a framework to decide whether or not to use a horse. It's another piece of evidence.

4. **Escalators (and de-escalators).** This pattern is also quite unusual. But particularly among younger horses, you occasionally see the kind of gradual, long-term, step-by-step improvement (or decline) exemplified in Windjammin Lady's past performances.

9 Windjammin Lady
Own:Lenci Anthony
Green Neon Pink Chevrons Pink L
CASTILLO O O (409 52 49 50 .13) 2002:(626 80 .13)

Ch. f. 3 (Mar) ONTSEP00 $8,804
Sire: Helmsman (El Gran Senor) $7,500
Dam: Loudoun Top(Feel the Power)
Br: Longview Farms (Ont-C)
Tr: Rogers J Michael(85 15 16 12 .18) 2002:(129 29 .22)

L 117

Life	12	3	4	1	$89,520	83	D.Fst	12	3	4	1	$89,520	83
2002	11	2	4	1	$79,260	83	Wet(290)	0	0	0	0	$0	–
2001	1	1	0	0	$10,260	60	Turf(250*)	0	0	0	0	$0	–
Del	6	1	3	0	$54,040	83	Dst(375)	10	3	4	0	$86,140	83

7Sep02-5Del	fst	6f	:22 :45^3 :58^3 1:12^2	3↑ ⒻAlw 61900N1X	77	4	3	2^{hd}	1½	1^{hd}	2^{nk}	Castillo O O	L 115 b	4.60	81-17	SusiB.Good118^{nk} WindjmmnLdy115^{2¼} Grshm115¾	Dueled,missed,2nd best	8
21Aug02-8Del	fst	6f	:22 :45^4 :59^1 1:12^1	3↑ ⒻAlw 44800N1X	59	5	6	5^{2¼}	5^{3½}	5^{1¾}	7^6	Castillo O O	L 114 b	*1.30	76-19	EtrnlOptmsm118^2 FblosFry114^{nk} ConcrdEscpd116½	Lacked needed rally	11
20Jly02-7Del	fst	6f	:22^1 :45^2 :58 1:11^1	ⒻAlw 40600N1X	83	6	5	4^{1¼}	2^{hd}	2^1	2no	Castillo O O	L 119 b	5.60	87-13	Lifbythdrop122^{no} WindjmmnLdy119^{hd} *Undrcovr*117^{nk}	Gamely, just missed	7
8Jly02-7Del	fst	6f	:22 :45^4 :58^4 1:12	3↑ ⒻAlw 39600N1X	78	5	1	2^{hd}	1^{hd}	3½	4^{3½}	Castillo O O	L 115 b	4.00	79-21	Ms.CDPlyr118^{hd} OutrightWgr118^2 ConcordEscpd113^{1½}	Dueled, weakened	7
11Jun02-8Del	fst	6f	:22 :45^1 :58 1:11^3	ⒻAlw 39600N1X	75	3	4	1^{hd}	1^{1½}	1^{1½}	2^1	Castillo O O	L 123 b	8.50	84-20	StyleChmp118^1 WindjmminLdy123^{1¾} AdorblJuli118^2	Held on stubbornly	7
27May02-6Del	fst	6f	:22^2 :46^3 1:00 1:13^4	ⒻClm 40000 (40-35)	70	1	3	1^{1½}	1^1	1^2	1^1	Castillo O O	L 118 b	4.20	74-21	Windjammin Lady118^1 Firing118^{nk} Umpateedle118^{5¼}	Steady drive	7
26Apr02-4Pim	fst	6f	:23^2 :47^1 :59^4 1:12^2	ⒻClm 35000 (35-30)	64	5	1	2^1	2^{1½}	2^{1½}	2^{2¾}	Castillo O O	L 119 b	5.50	80-15	*BluCrk*117^{2¾} *WindjmminLdy*119^{1¾} AmriPrincss117^1	Chased off rail,willng	7
7Apr02-7Pim	fst	1$\frac{1}{16}$	:23^2 :47^1 1:12^4 1:46	ⒻAlw 26000N1X	54	9	2^1	2½	2^1	6^{9½}	6^{14}	Castillo O O	L 117 b	5.30	63-24	BroadPicture122^{3¾} ClickOnMe117^{no} *GloriousCt*117^{3¾}	3wd early, weakened	9
24Mar02-6Lrl	fst	6f	:22 :45^1 :57^4 1:10^4	ⒻAlw 26000N1X	42	6	7	7^{12}	7^{14}	6^{12}	4^{13¼}	Castillo O O	117	4.50	72-19	*Gzillion*122^1 Cottonpickinminute117^1 TownScrt117^{11}	Passed tiring rivals	8
2Mar02-2Lrl	fst	6f	:23^2 :48 1:00^3 1:13^3	ⒻClm c-(35-30)	53	3	7	7^{2½}	7^{2½}	5^{2¼}	1no	Pino M G	117	*2.70	71-25	WndjmmnLdy117^{no} NEsyAnsr119^{hd} RllySmth113^{1¼}	Easd bck 1/2,5wd surge	8

Claimed from Fitzgerald Shelley E for $35,000, Wilcox Warren Trainer 2002(as of 03/02): (24 4 1 3 0.17)
WORKS: Aug10 Del 5f fst 1:02 B *3/8*
TRAINER: Dirt(249 .21 $2.25) Sprint(182 .21 $2.19) Alw(57 .18 $2.15)

Ironically, as soon as the public bet her down to 6-5 on August 21—after a remarkable six consecutive improvements in her Beyer figures, and after her most draining effort—she finally tossed in a bad one. Why? I'm afraid nobody could answer that with any authority.

5. Cyclers. This is a much more widespread pattern, involving a series of improving figures—for example, 55-63-75—followed by a bounce to 51, a rebound to 65, and a return to a figure in the mid-to-upper 70's. A complete cycle. When these horses peak and decline, you can try to catch them when their Beyers begin to improve again. Many of the horses described as "three-and-out" types by Andrew Beyer would fit into this group. But you'll also find some who are "four-and-out" or even "five-and-out." Many of these horses will continue to improve and decline in stages, sometimes for months at a time. And for the significant number that follow this cycling pattern up to their previous high Beyers, you often get tremendous odds because their best races are well buried, four or five lines deep in their past performances. Even if they don't win, these types can give you a high-priced filler in the second, third, or fourth slot in exactas, trifectas, or superfectas. As we will see, the cycling pattern is by far the most valuable of all the patterns you might discover in a horse's form.

Why do some horses run in these patterns? Who knows? There's no real explanation for it. And some horses will develop multiple-pattern personalities. They will be repeat-figure performers for six consecutive races in June and July, and then in October and November they will change completely and go through a perfect three-and-out cycle. Same horse, different time, different pattern—as in the case of Linus:

These patterns are always temporary, limited to a particular short span of time—usually only a matter of weeks or months. So they can't be explained by something inherent in a horse's permanent physical makeup—biorhythms, or some such thing. And they can't all be explained away by analyzing the trips or track conditions encountered in each race. There's an element of mystery in all this, something we can't really explain. But its value for handicapping is no mystery. It's real and demonstrable.

10 Noles
Own: Team Central Inc
Red, Yellow '226' On Black Ball
CARABALLO J C (472 63 69 75 .13) 2002:(838 111 .13)

Dk. b or br c. 3 (Mar)
Sire: Mountain Cat (Storm Cat) $15,000
Dam: Gold 'n Desire(Gold and Myrrh)
Br: Richard Joseph Troncone (Ky)
Tr: Lake Scott A(284 74 47 31 .26) 2002:(1464 322 .22)

L 117

Life	23	6	5	5	$138,450	88	D.Fst	21	6	4	4	$128,720 88
2002	17	6	3	4	$124,210	88	Wet(335)	2	0	1	1	$9,730 84
2001	6	M	2	1	$14,240	62	Turf(230)	0	0	0	0	$0 –
Del	10	3	3	2	$91,040	88	Dst(325)	9	2	3	2	$63,660 88

19Oct02-9Del	wf	6f	:213	:45	:574	1:11	3↑ Alw 44200N1X	**84**	3	4	31½	32	22½	31¾	Potts C L	L 120 b	*2.00	86-11	*Orka*115nk **My Good Trick**1151½ Noles1201½	Outfinished late	9
10Oct02-1Del	fst	6f	:213	:441	:57	1:103	Clm 35000(35-30)	**88**	6	1	44	35	22½	11	Potts C L	L 117 b	*2.40	90-09	Noles1171 Lennon1122¾ *Orka*113nk	Wore down leader	6
18Sep02-6Del	fst	6f	:214	:453	:59	1:124	Clm 25000(25-20)	**75**	7	5	56	42¾	1hd	1¾	Potts C L	L 117 b	4.20	79-19	*Noles*117¾ Radio One117no Lennon1173½	Rail bid, hard drive	9
3Sep02-7Del	fst	170	:231	:471	1:123	1:431	Alw 43300N1X	**57**	6	42½	32	31½	44	415¾	Potts C L	L 115 b	2.60	69-22	*Private Lap*1173 Mt. Moran1155½ Vid Alert1207½	Well placed, no rally	6
14Aug02-7Del	fst	1 1/16	:234	:483	1:142	1:47	Alw 40600N1X	**73**	7	21½	31½	2hd	12½	25¾	McCarthy M J	L 117 b	2.30	67-28	Morgan Dollar1175¾ Noles1172 Jule Bandit1172¾	No match,bested rest	7
3Aug02-8Del	fst	170	:232	:474	1:131	1:44	Alw 40600N1X	**77**	6	11	1½	1hd	12½	21	McCarthy M J	L 117 b	2.60	80-17	*Make The Bend*1171 Noles1171½ Chain1175¾	Pace, not good enough	7
13Jly02-6Del	fst	170	:234	:481	1:14	1:442	Clm c-(16-14)	**86**	3	1½	11½	11½	15	110½	Black A S	L 117 b	*1.50	79-28	Noles11710 Charles119½ Corrider's Choice1174½	Repulsed bid, drew off	7
Claimed from Evola Russell for $16,000, Cataldi Tony Trainer 2002(as of 07/13): (99 17 16 16 0.17) Previously trained by Peterson Michael J																					
18Jun02-6Del	fst	6f	:22	:46	:584	1:114	3↑ Clm 25000(25-20)	**72**	9	1	73¼	31	33	55	Bracho J A	L 115 fb	21.90	79-15	Quick Punch1183½ Golden O's120nk Euroclydon118no	Bid, flattened out	9
21May02-5Del	fst	1	:242	:482	1:142	1:411	Clm 20000(20-18)	**65**	6	21	21	2hd	1hd	35½	Bracho J A	L 116 b	4.90	70-24	I've Got The Time1165½ Mt. Moran116hd Noles1166¼	Came in, weakened	7
12May02-3Del	wf	6f	:223	:461	:583	1:104	Clm c-(16-14)	**80**	2	3	1hd	1hd	12	2½	Rose J	L 119 b	*1.90	88-13	Twining Moment116½ Noles1199 Sweep TheShore1161½	Just failed to last	5
Claimed from Turner Edward E for $16,000, Hartsell John J Jr Trainer 2002(as of 05/12): (44 7 9 5 0.16)																					

TRAINER: Dirt(2806 .25 $1.73) Sprint(1994 .26 $1.88) Alw(784 .21 $1.62)

Noles could be the national poster boy for Beyer Speed Figure cycling. Since the late winter he had been reliably running up and down the Beyer scale. On October 19 he had the clear top Beyer figure in a field of nine allowance sprinters. If he continued to follow the remarkably symmetrical, graphlike contour of his Beyer figures, he would decline substantially in this race.

The race set up perfectly for Noles. Two horses dueled in vicious fractions while he sat behind them on the turn. By mid-turn you already could see he was struggling. He couldn't keep up at all until he finally began to gain some ground late on the turn. He closed mildly in the stretch but flattened out late and finished third. His Beyer only dropped to 84—not as far as I would have anticipated, but then he did have a perfect trip. And his persistent cycling continued.

In that same race was My Good Trick, who was approaching the top of his cycle.

11 My Good Trick
Own: Gill Michael J
Blue, Blue 'cmmmc' On White Ball
ALVARADO F T (5 0 1 0 .00) 2002:(811 93 .11)

Dk. b or br g. 3 (Mar)
Sire: Tricky Fun (Phone Trick) $2,000
Dam: Some Kinda Good(Preemptive)
Br: Jim Lorenz (Ark)
Tr: Shuman Mark(467 64 78 64 .14) 2002:(645 97 .15)

L 115

Life	16	4	3	4	$89,175	87	D.Fst	12	3	2	3	$66,075	87
2002	11	3	2	2	$72,795	87	Wet(355*)	3	1	1	1	$23,100	87
2001	5	1	1	2	$16,380	67	Turf(290*)	1	0	0	0	$0	52
Del	5	1	2	0	$40,900	87	Dst(365)	12	4	3	4	$87,975	87

19Oct02-9Del wf 6f :213 :45 :574 1:11 3↑ Alw 44200N1X **87** 2 7 76 63 44½ 2nk Rose J L 115 b 4.30 88-11 *Orka*115nk My Good Trick1151½ **Noles**1201½ Closed fast, missed 9
5Oct02-5Del fst 6f :22 :451 :581 1:111 3↑ Alw 43600N1X **78** 1 7 76 75½ 34½ 21½ Rose J L 115 b 6.90 85-13 ResonToHil1181½ MyGoodTrick1153¼ JosGspr120nk Bumped rival,clsd fast 7
27Aug02-7Del fst 6f :221 :46 :582 1:104 Alw 44200N1X **48** 4 6 94¾ 74¼ 78½ 716 Johnston M T L 119 b 5.10 73-17 *Safe In The U S A*117½ Chain1177¼ Kylemore Abbey117hd Showed little 9
3Aug02-8Del fst 170 :232 :474 1:131 1:44 Alw 40600N1X **64** 4 21 31 31 56 58¾ Johnston M T L 117 b *2.00 72-17 *Make The Bend*1171 **Noles**1171¼ Chain1175¾ Stalked, bid, tired 7
24Jly02-4Del fst 6f :221 :46 :584 1:112 Clm c-(35-30) **87** 5 5 52¾ 42¾ 1hd 12¾ Dominguez R A L 117 b *2.30 86-20 MyGodTrck1172¾ TwnngMmnt1171½ SthrnLvn1171¾ Rail, came out, closed 7
Claimed from Englander Richard A for $35,000, Pino Michael V Trainer 2002(as of 07/24): (171 47 23 20 0.27) Previously trained by Asmussen Steven M
23May02-8LS fm 5f Ⓣ :223 :451 :571 Alw 28000N1X **52** 4 10 910 99 913 87¾ Lanerie C J L 116 b 10.40 86-06 ThreeJck116hd Engrved1162 XtremeMoniqu116½ Broke in, saved ground 10
10Apr02-10OP fst 5½f :213 :453 :581 1:043 3↑ [S]OClm 20000N **66** 5 2 23 3nk 31 77¼ Lopez J L 117 b *1.70 86-14 I'mMajestic1183 RobeByou1161 BlueExplosion118nk Bid between, faded 10
30Mar02-7OP sly 6f :22 :461 :584 1:12 [S]Rainbow61k **80** 11 3 21½ 21 34½ 36 St Julien M L 116 b 1.80 74-21 *PrfctFntsy*1195 *SnowbllKing*1151 MyGoodTrck1163¾ Forward, even drive 11
4Mar02-1FG fst 6f :214 :451 :573 1:101 Clm c-50000 **80** 2 3 2hd 1hd 2hd 34 Martin E M Jr L 119 b *.60 86-13 Garb1173½ Timeless Buy117½ My Good Trick1196½ Edge, faltered late 5
Claimed from Tom Boy Stable for $50,000, Amoss Thomas Trainer 2002(as of 03/04): (95 32 13 16 0.34)
18Feb02-6FG fst 6f :212 :451 :572 1:103 Clm 50000 **85** 3 3 2hd 1hd 1hd 14 Martin E M Jr L 117 b 2.00 88-15 MyGoodTrick1174 Yippee1172 HunterInThSky119½ Shook off, drew out 6
WORKS: ●Sep9 Del 4f fst :492 B *1/19*
TRAINER: Dirt(666 .15 $1.50) Sprint(346 .14 $1.76) Alw(168 .13 $1.08)

While Noles had run an 88 in his previous race and looked about to bounce, My Good Trick had run an 87 back on July 24 and appeared to be improving again up to that level. Noles was 2-1, My Good Trick was 4-1. In the October 19 race, My Good Trick ran right past the struggling Noles late in the stretch and did indeed improve again to an 87 Beyer. Unfortunately, he couldn't catch the winner, who dueled and then amazingly held on by a desperate neck. I could explain Noles and My Good Trick, but I couldn't explain the winner's remarkable performance. And so it sometimes goes in this game.

The near-perfect, repetitive symmetry of Noles's past performances is rare in Thoroughbred racing. Form is seldom so mechanistic, so predictable. But the overall shape of Noles's speed-figure pattern is not just a racing oddity. It is worth a long look for two reasons. First, it represents the concept of cycling in its ideal form. It is the very definition of cycling speed figures. And second, there are enough cases similar, if not identical, to that of Noles to make this angle a worthwhile tool. These horses often provide tremendous value to players alert to this pattern. As mentioned above, the value in these runners comes from the simple fact that their best efforts are three or four races back (as was the case with My Good Trick), and so they avoid that too-exclusive focus of too many players on a recent strong effort, a sure killer of parimutuel value.

The logic behind this angle is equally simple, and is related to the reasoning behind the bounce. A horse puts in a peak effort after a pattern of improvement, and it takes something out of him physically. He reacts. His next race reflects that draining effort, and he runs poorly. Then, in his subsequent start, he begins to rebound, improving his Beyers in the direction of his earlier best effort. Finally, he is ready to repeat his peak performance, or at least approach it—and sometimes even surpass it. That's the cycle: big race, bounce, recovery, and then a big effort again.

As we have already emphasized, this pattern applies only to a certain number of horses—and only at certain times in their racing careers. And there are an endless number of variations even within this cycling theme—many of them not nearly as clear-cut as the example of Noles. In addition, not every pattern that *appears* to be a cycle is worth following. There are a number of warning signs you should watch for in order to avoid using these horses when a deeper look shows that they don't warrant your support:

- Beware of horses with cycling figures who have recent sharp drops in class, or long gaps in their form. These might indicate some physical problem that will prevent the horse from returning to his best form.
- The peak race you are projecting the horse to repeat should not be more than two or three months in the past. Farther back than that and you are, for all practical purposes, dealing with a very different horse.
- You still have to make sure that, in the race you're handicapping, the horse is at the right distance and on the proper surface.
- Most importantly, the figure you can reasonably project as the horse's best must be competitive with the field he is currently facing. After all, a horse that is cycling well short of his competitors' figures is not worth much to the bettor.

If you find a horse who avoids any of these potential negatives, and appears to be cycling up to a much better effort, you have a horse worth using—and often at a big price. The fifth race at Delaware on August 3 was living proof.

The key to this race was the front-runner, Pleasantly Rich. He was the clear speed in an otherwise paceless seven-horse claimer at the $12,500 level. He looked tough to beat at 6-5. Who would complete the exacta? On the surface it looked like a wide-open scramble for second, with everything from a layoff California shipper, to a slight drop-down, to a recent claim, to a $9,000 claimer moving up after running improved Beyers in three consecutive races—a potential bounce candidate. All these horses frequently ran Beyers in the mid-to-upper 70's, so it was hard to separate them. But the most intriguing possibility for second was Core Idea.

He had three big positives. First, he had a promising cycling pattern in his Beyer Speed Figures. After a hard-earned 81 back on May 19, Core Idea had bounced all the way down to a 52, and, after a very brief rest, had improved to a 65 in his last start. If he could continue to improve toward that earlier 81, he would have an excellent shot at the place behind Pleasantly Rich. Second, he had more speed than most of the field, so he would have a better tactical position close to the front-runner in what figured to be a slow-paced race. And third, because his previous figure was only a 65 and his last two races looked rather dull on paper, he was totally ignored in the betting.

The race unfolded according to plan, with Pleasantly Rich galloping off by himself, and widening his margin in the stretch. He was never threatened. And Core Idea finished a clear second, completing an exacta of $64.80. If you were not attuned to the cycling pattern, you would never think of using a horse like Core Idea. His recent form just looked too dull. For these types—when you're using them only because of a projection based on the Beyers—you should demand solid value in return. And Core Idea was certainly big value.

Value was the key to another cycler, Starry De. In the George Rosenberger Memorial at Delaware on September 7, this filly was part of a field in which five runners had recorded Beyers between 91 and 94 in their most recent races. It looked like a hopeless tangle. A horse named High Lady had the top figure from a race on July 8, had a good post position, and was trained by a solid conditioner. High Lady looked like a must-use at 5-1. But the key to the race was the value horse, Starry De. She was just as capable of running in the low 90's as the other five contenders, but her 92 was well hidden back in her form.

Starry De
Own: Jester Michael W

B. m. 4 KEESEP99 $57,000
Sire: Star de Naskra (Naskra) $10,000
Dam: Sweepy(Icecapade)
Br: Fairview Farm (Ky)
Tr: Rogers J Michael (—) 2002:(201 32 .16)

Life	18	3	3	5	$131,805	92	D.Fst	10	2	2	3	$75,030	79
2002	8	2	1	2	$85,235	92	Wet(345)	0	0	0	0	$0	–
2001	8	0	2	2	$25,490	80	Turf(250)	8	1	1	2	$56,775	92
CSC	0	0	0	0	$0	–	Dist	0	0	0	0	$0	–

7Sep02-9Del	fm	1 1/16	Ⓣ	:243 :482 1:122 1:422	3↑ Ⓕ[R]GRosnbrgrMem101k	91	7	1½	11½	1hd	2hd	31	Castillo O O	L 114 f	19.70	94–04	High Lady1161 Bloomy114hd Starry De114½	Disputed pace,hung	11
18Aug02-7Del	fst	1		:234 :473 1:134 1:414	3↑ ⒻOClm 50000N	72	6	67	63¾	54	32½	33¾	Castillo O O	L 118	4.30	69–27	DnceTheSlew1233 ProspectRunner118¾ StrryDe1181½	Mid m,wknd drive	7
Previously trained by Schettino Dominick A																			
29Jly02-6Sar	fm	1⅛	Ⓣ	:461 1:101 1:343 1:472	3↑ ⒻAlw 52000N3X	62	6	75¾	68½	76½	87¾	814¾	Luzzi M J	L 119	15.30	77–10	Unbridled Vice1172 *Love N' Kiss S.*117nk Dulcito1181	Tired	8
24Jun02-7Del	fm	1⅛	Ⓣ	:482 1:12 1:363 1:484	3↑ ⒻNew Castle H100k	81	3	32	31½	32	61¾	56½	Castillo O O	L 113	11.90	90–05	Lady Of The Future114¾ [D]Salty You113¾ *Calista*116¾	Failed to respond	6
8Jun02-8Del	fm	1 1/16	Ⓣ	:24 :48 1:113 1:423	3↑ ⒻRosenna76k	92	9	53	66¼	64	52	4½	Castillo O O	L 119	17.50	93–08	Rhum115no Morena Park115no De Aar115½	Needed closing bid	10
21Apr02-7Aqu	yl	1 1/16	Ⓣ	:244 :501 1:143 1:452	3↑ ⒻAlw 46000N2X	88	6	31½	31	3½	2hd	1¾	Luzzi M J	L 121	10.90	77–19	Starry De121¾ Ready1231¼ Getadderit121½	Stumbled start, bumped	9
28Mar02-6Aqu	fst	1⅛		:482 1:13 1:381 1:512	4↑ ⒻAlw 44000N1X	79	2	52	51½	42¼	11	12	Velazquez J R	L 118	3.30	79–20	*Starry De*1182 Home Deed1184 Darling Bride1202¾	Quick 4 wide move	8
17Jan02-9Aqu	fst	1	⊡	:234 :474 1:133 1:40	4↑ ⒻAlw 44000N2L	74	3	88½	89	75	33	21¼	Lezcano L5	L 112	3.60	77–30	ThNumbrsAddUp1171¼ *StrryD*112hd *SbrOfSlvr*112hd	Stumbled start, 5 wide	10
19Dec01-8Aqu	fst	1	⊡	:234 :474 1:123 1:392	3↑ ⒻAlw 44000N2L	73	4	75	74¾	63	31½	31¼	Castillo H Jr	L 116	7.20	80–24	FoxyRed116nk Emily'sPlesure1161 [DH]StrryD116	Steadied into bckstrch	9
Previously trained by Sumja Brent																			
3Nov01-8Aqu	fm	1 1/16	Ⓣ	:232 :483 1:133 1:444	3↑ ⒻAlw 44000N1X	74	10	41¾	32	31	63¼	75¼	Castillo H Jr	L 116 b	6.50	75–15	PeanutGllery1191½ AmericnDremer1161¼ TCKiss116no	Chased 3 wide, tired	10

On June 8 Starry De had closed well to run her top lifetime figure. Then she went straight backward, turning in declining Beyers of 81 and then 62. She began to rebound in a dirt race on August 18 with a Beyer of 72. If she could cycle back up to her earlier Beyer in the low 90's, she would put herself in the mix. And she went off at 19-1. Starry De dictated the pace in this race, setting comfortable fractions. She dug in gamely when challenged in the stretch, but she couldn't withstand the charge of High Lady. Unfortunately, she lost the place by a head in the final jump, blowing a life-enhancing exacta of 5-1 and 19-1. Still, with the second finisher also among the possible contenders, Starry De was the key to a very haveable trifecta worth $1,197.20.

It goes without saying that, like every other isolated approach to handicapping, projecting improvement based solely on figure patterns does not always work. It has its fair share of disappointments. But it can give you what many other approaches cannot: live horses at long prices. And, ultimately, that's the name of the game: It is not about appearing more clever, or sounding more sophisticated, or picking more winners than the next guy. The name of the game is making money, and these live cycling horses can contribute in a big way.

Take the example of the talented grass gelding Berchtesgaden:

Back in 2001 Berchtesgaden had displayed a cycling pattern when, after a figure of 93 on May 19, he had dropped down to a 48 in his next start, only to rebound to an 89 and then back up to a 95, losing by only a half-length at odds of nearly 20-1. On April 19 of 2002 he returned to the races with a tough wide trip and a big figure of 95. He bounced to a 68, hindered by breaking a bit slow and being hung out wide again. Then he repeated the pattern from 2001, improving to a 90 in his next start. A sloppy track then interrupted any potential cycle. If you believed Berchtesgaden could still return to a figure in the 95 range on the grass, you were right. On July 4 he broke from the very unfavorable 10 post at 1¼ miles on the Belmont inner turf, chased the pace in the two path the whole way, and hung on very gamely to lose by only one length. And he was 14-1.

Here are five other classic cases of successful cyclers:

10 Runspastum
Own:Jayeff B Stables
Burnt Orange, Turquoise Belt, Turquoise
MCCARTHY M J (5 0 0 0 .00) 2002:(792 136 .17)
B. h. 5
Sire: Woodman (Mr. Prospector) $40,000
Dam: Erandel(Danzig)
Br: Calumet Farm (Ky)
Tr: Goldberg Alan E(7 1 1 0 .14) 2002:(144 24 .17)
L 114

Life	29	6	6	4	$472,624	105	D.Fst	19 4 5 2	$308,194	105
2002	9	1	3	2	$158,120	105	Wet(345)	3 1 1 0	$112,880	105
2001	9	2	2	1	$146,364	105	Turf(295)	7 1 0 2	$51,550	96
Med	2	0	1	0	$20,300	90	Dst(320)	7 3 0 1	$239,840	105

7Sep02-7Del fst 1⅛ :464 1:113 1:381 1:511 3↑ ⓇOwners'Day H100k 104 5 75½ 73½ 55 42 13 McCarthy M J L119 b *1.90 90-14 Runspastum1193 AmericanPrince115½ ConfuciusSy1191¾ Blocked,split h 8
18Aug02-10Mth fst 1⅛ :471 1:103 1:36 1:49 3↑ PH Iselin H-G2 105 7 53 54½ 44 31½ 31 Pimentel J L114 b 37.10 94-11 **Ct'sAtHom**116¾ **Bowmn'sBnd**117nk *Runspstm*1144¼ Finished well outside 7
20Jly02-4Del fst 1 1/16 :23 :453 1:101 1:424 3↑ RRMCrpterJrM100k 101 7 711 711 63½ 44 34 McCarthy M J L116 fb 24.30 90-11 **Bowmn'sBnd**1162¼ *Grundlfoot*1231¾ Runspstum1164¼ Rated, bid, easily 3rd 7
29Jun02-7Del fst 1 :241 :474 1:121 1:371 3↑ Brandywine100k 92 4 54½ 66½ 57 511 411 Castillo O O L116 b 8.50 85-20 He's A Knockout1163 Marciano1167¾ Beau's Surprise116hd Evenly 7
15Jun02-10Mth my 1 1/16 ⊗ :241 :474 1:111 1:423 3↑ Oceanport H91k 105 3 32½ 2½ 21 22 23 Lopez C C L112 fb 1.00 92-16 TmpstFugt1153 Runspstum1128¼ OnEydJokr114 Threatened,gave chase 3
5May02-6Del fst 1 1/16 :232 :47 1:112 1:433 3↑ Alw 52000N$mY 102 2 45 46½ 44 33 2½ McCarthy M J L115 b *1.10 89-17 First Amendment120½ Runspastum1155 Lyracist1202 Closed,too late 5
22Mar02-8Aqu fst 1⅛ :471 1:104 1:36 1:492 4↑ Alw 54000C 98 7 64½ 68½ 67½ 58 41¾ Arroyo N Jr L118 b 3.20 87-26 Jarf123nk *John Little*1181 Mike's Thunder116½ Good finish outside 9
21Feb02-8Aqu fst 1 ⊡ :243 :483 1:123 1:364 4↑ Alw 54000C 101 6 42½ 3½ 2hd 21½ 2½ Arroyo N Jr L118 b 7.10 93-26 *Jarf*118½ Runspastum1182½ John Little1182¾ Game finish outside 8
5Jan02-7Aqu fst 170 ⊡ :234 :472 1:112 1:393 4↑ Alw 56000C 93 7 75¼ 75½ 63¾ 59½ 59¾ Arroyo N Jr L118 b 8.10 86-22 BostonParty118½ AffirmedSuccess1235½ Basil'sRhythm116no Had no rally 7
1Dec01-8Aqu fst 1 3/16 :484 1:113 1:36 1:55 3↑ QueensCntyH-G3 96 6 44½ 45½ 45½ 46½ 46 Arroyo N Jr L114 b 7.20 96-08 *EveningAttire*1131¾ BaltoStar1182¼ TopOfficial1132 Close up, no response 8
TRAINER: Dirt(245 .20 $1.65) Routes(188 .19 $1.74) GrdStk(20 .15 $1.11)

9 Misspent
Own:Imbesi Joseph M
White, Green Cross Sashes, Red B, Red
$75,000
PIMENTEL J (8 1 0 1 .13) 2002:(479 53 .11)
Gr/ro m. 5
Sire: Two Punch (Mr. Prospector) $25,000
Dam: La Santa(Sunny's Halo)
Br: Joseph M Imbesi (NJ)
Tr: Aristone Philip T (—) 2002:(242 45 .19)
L 120

Life	18	5	2	2	$170,557	84	D.Fst	17 5 2 2	$170,157	84
2002	8	2	1	1	$60,452	84	Wet(355)	0 0 0 0	$0	–
2001	10	3	1	1	$110,105	78	Turf(195)	1 0 0 0	$400	55
Aqu	0	0	0	0	$0	–	Dst(315)	0 0 0 0	$0	–

Previously trained by Woodington Jamie
21Sep02-7Pim fst 6f :224 :453 :58 1:111 3↑ ⒻⓇMdMillDstfH95k 63 10 4 42½ 44 1013 1012 Pimentel J L114 14.60e 77-13 BlindedByLove1153¼ CseOfThBlus1201 Grcfulciti114nk Wide 1/2, gave way 11
28Aug02-8Mth fst 6f :214 :444 :571 1:101 3↑ ⒻⓈElevenNorthH50k 73 3 3 3½ 21½ 24 49 Velez J A Jr L120 4.80 79-15 GoldenMde1217¾ Mry'sNickle119nk SilntSrnd1221 2deep,angled in,weaknd 5
Previously trained by Preciado Guadalupe
9Aug02-7Mth fst 6f :214 :444 :571 1:102 3↑ ⒻOClm 35000 (35-30)N 84 1 6 2hd 41¼ 31 11¼ Elliott S L122 5.70 87-15 Misspent1221¼ Tempura120nk Miss Marni1173 Moved outside,drvg 7
26Jly02-8Mth fst 6f :214 :444 :572 1:103 3↑ ⒻOClm 35000 (35-30)N 75 6 2 2hd 1hd 11 1¾ Velez J A Jr L120 4.90e 86-19 *Misspent*120¾ Delta Quick120½ Prime Juice1202 Charged gate,kept driv 9
12Jly02-8Mth fst 6f :214 :451 1:104 3↑ ⒻAlw 35000N2X 53 8 4 73¾ 52½ 74¼ 79 Beckner D V L120 3.80 76-21 Mary's Nickle1202¼ Fit Performer120½ Tempura1203¾ Outside,widest turn 8
25Jun02-7Del fst 6f :214 :451 :574 1:104 3↑ ⒻLateBloomer63k 70 5 10 55 64¼ 64½ 79¼ Beckner D V L116 18.10 80-15 UrbnDncer1163 DivineLin116¾ OutstndingInfo123nk Gradually weakened 11
26May02-9Mth fst 6f :222 :46 :582 1:111 3↑ ⓈAlw 48250N3X 83 3 5 3nk 1hd 3nk 33 Beckner D V L115 2.70 80-22 Vow1203 Lyle Lovesit120hd Misspent115no Pressed,led,not enough 10
11May02-10Mth fst 6f :214 :45 :572 1:103 3↑ ⒻⓈOpen Mind H50k 79 6 2 41½ 21 22 24¼ Beckner D V L115 5.60 82-17 SilentSerende1184¼ Misspnt1156½ NowListnSistr116½ 3 wide, second best 9
1Nov01-9Med fst 6f :22 :45 :573 1:10 3↑ ⒻⓈAlw 60000N2X 78 10 1 51½ 41½ 1hd 14¾ Pimentel J5 L115 *1.50e 89-15 Misspent1154¾ Missbehviour113no MyDncinGirl1181¼ Angled in, drew clear 10
13Oct01-9Med fst 6f :213 :441 :564 1:094 3↑ ⓈAlw 60000N2X 64 4 8 64¼ 55½ 63¼ 45 Pimentel J5 L113 14.20 85-09 Vow1181¾ Given To Fly111½ *Belong To Who*1192¾ Steadied midstretch 11
4Oct01-8Med fst 6f :221 :452 :58 1:111 3↑ ⒻⓈAlw 50000N1X 64 2 5 42½ 56½ 43 12½ Pimentel J5 L113 *1.60 83-16 Misspent1132½ Dear Prospector118¾ LeadingLena118no Angled out,rallied 9
Previously trained by Sacco Gregory D
26Sep01-8Med yl 5f Ⓣ :223 :464 :594 3↑ ⒻAlw 40000N1X 55 10 3 84½ 96¾ 106½ 96½ Carrero V5 L118 29.90 70-24 Cloud City114¾ Always On The Go115nk Gotta Be A Star115½ Outrun 10
WORKS: Oct14 Pha 5f gd 1:012 B *1/1* Sep10 Mth 6f fst 1:14 B *1/2*
TRAINER: 1stW/Tm(45 .09 $0.62) 31-60Days(30 .20 $2.51) Dirt(373 .17 $1.38) Sprint(209 .16 $1.30) Claim(283 .19 $1.60)

2 This Guns For Hire
Own:Frassetto Albert
Light Blue, Yellow Diamond Frame, Yellow
MIGLIORE R (8 2 2 3 .25) 2002:(734 115 .16)
B. c. 3 (Mar) EASOCT00 $23,000
Sire: Norquestor (Conquistador Cielo) $5,000
Dam: Dr. Nunn(Mt. Livermore)
Br: Mr & Mrs Charles McGinnes (Md)
Tr: Terranova John P II (—) 2002:(109 14 .13)
L 115

Life	8	2	4	2	$99,620	98	D.Fst	7 2 3 2	$91,020	98
2002	8	2	4	2	$99,620	98	Wet(425)	1 0 1 0	$8,600	79
2001	0	M	0	0	$0	–	Turf(310)	0 0 0 0	$0	–
Med	0	0	0	0	$0	–	Dst(340)	2 2 0 0	$56,400	96

28Aug02-8Sar fst 1⅛ :473 1:123 1:38 1:512 3↑ Alw 48000N1X 94 7 2½ 2hd 2hd 1½ 12 Velazquez J R L119 4.20 82-18 ThsGunsForHr1192 Dr.Rocktt1171 FshrPond1173½ Speed outside, driving 7
1Aug02-4Sar fst 1⅛ :474 1:122 1:373 1:511 3↑ Md Sp Wt 46k 96 3 1½ 11 11 14½ 12¾ Migliore R L119 2.70 83-25 *ThisGunsForHr*1192¾ *Volkonsky*1191¾ SnglRnbow1194 Pace, clear, driving 11
7Jly02-2Bel fst 1 1/16 :224 :451 1:101 1:434 3↑ Md Sp Wt 44k 82 2 4¾ 2hd 12½ 12 21½ Migliore R L119 f 2.60 79-13 GoldenSlew1141½ *ThisGunsForHir*11910 ForignAuthority1192½ Outfinished 7
15Jun02-1Bel sly 7f :222 :452 1:094 1:223 3↑ Md Sp Wt 43k 79 3 3 32 3½ 21½ 23¾ Migliore R L120 f *.45 86-10 OrSmmrStrm1153¾ ThsGnsFrHr1204 SngngSmm1207½ 3 wide, second best 6
8May02-2Bel fst 7f :223 :454 1:10 1:224 3↑ Md Sp Wt 43k 98 6 4 43 2½ 2hd 2½ Migliore R L120 f .80e 88-15 SovrignSwp120½ ThisGunsForHir1207½ Addicks1201 Game finish outside 6
11Apr02-3Aqu fst 7f :23 :462 1:102 1:23 Md Sp Wt 41k 87 2 4 42 31 22 22¼ Migliore R L120 f 3.65 83-17 **RegalSnction**1202¼ ThisGunsForHire1203½ Tourist1209¼ Game finish inside 5
16Mar02-6Aqu fst 7f :23 :464 1:124 1:254 Md Sp Wt 41k 67 2 6 31½ 31 31 33¼ Gryder A T L120 fb *.95 68-23 Gico1203¼ Strtchyourfith120no ThsGunsForHr1202¼ 3 wide move, no punch 8
21Jan02-6Aqu fst 6f ⊡ :231 :463 :583 1:111 Md Sp Wt 41k 71 2 5 33 42 36½ 34¼ Gryder A T L120 fb 7.30 84-12 JrsyGint1203½ *Smokin'John*120¾ ThsGunsForHr1202 Chased inside, tired 9
WORKS: Sep21 Bel 5f fst :593 B *2/37* Sep15 Bel 5f fst :594 H *2/20* Sep10 Bel 4f fst :493 B *13/28* Aug19 Sar 5f fst 1:01 B *7/37* Jly28 Sar 5f fst :593 H *2/34* Jly22 Sar 5f fst 1:013 B *4/17*
TRAINER: Dirt(202 .15 $1.49) Routes(103 .11 $0.79) GrdStk(27 .04 $0.38)

5 Miles River
Own:D A S L Stable
Purple, Purple 'dasl' On Gold Ball
$5,000
POTTS C L (735 130 105 89 .18) 2002:(757 133 .18)
Ch. h. 5
Sire: Eastern Echo (Damascus) $3,000
Dam: Dame Capote(Capote)
Br: Stonerside Stable Ltd (Ky)
Tr: Wasserman Richard A(4 1 1 0 .25) 2002:(75 9 .12)
L 120

Life	48	11	7	3	$121,596	87	D.Fst	37 8 5 3	$95,456	84
2002	16	6	4	1	$35,410	75	Wet(365)	8 3 2 0	$25,480	87
2001	17	2	0	1	$21,286	80	Turf(270)	3 0 0 0	$660	69
Del	4	1	2	0	$20,100	87	Dst(300)	19 5 4 2	$58,513	87

3Nov02-1Del fst 1 :24 :48 1:142 1:411 3↑ Clm 5000 74 2 22 21½ 2½ 11½ 11¾ Rose J L118 fb 8.70 76-23 Miles River1181¾ **Vilar**1182¾ Retro Fever1181½ Sharply roused 9
23Oct02-7Pen fst 170 :231 :472 1:131 1:444 3↑ Clm 6250 (6.25-6)N2Y 50 1 11 1½ 1½ 34½ 613¾ Portillo D A L117 fb 6.00 64-26 Hands To The Side1163¼ King Oro1171 *Nine Iron*1163¼ Stopped inside 7
27Sep02-7CT sly 1⅛ :471 1:13 1:401 1:542 3↑ Clm 7500 (7.5-7) 18 5 31 43 410 819 840 Kravets J L116 fb *2.60 38-33 Eastover1167½ Majestic Irish1161½ Crebilly1165 Hard used 1/2, stopped 8
31Aug02-1Del fst 170 :242 :49 1:15 1:451 3↑ Clm 6250 (6.25-6) 68 5 2½ 2½ 1½ 2½ 2½ Salvaggio M V L118 fb 3.90 74-23 AllnsMoney118½ MilesRiver1183¾ *SwiftTrms*118½ Bore in st,dueled,hung 7
14Aug02-9Pen fst 170 :223 :464 1:111 1:42 3↑ Clm 5000 75 3 36½ 32½ 11 15 18¼ Salvaggio M V L116 fb *2.10 92-10 Miles River1168¼ *Battenberg*1166 Jennys Badboy1162½ 3 wide, driving 6
28Jly02-7Pha fst 170 :232 :471 1:13 1:451 3↑ Clm 5000 57 6 2½ 2½ 1hd 41½ 37¼ Flores J L L120 fb 4.40 69-29 HenbneMn1154¼ SpeedyEscort1203 *MilesRivr*1204½ Pressed,bid,weakened 6
13Jly02-4Pen fst 1 1/16 :24 :481 1:13 1:47 3↑ Clm 5000 58 4 812 810 710 68¼ 56¾ Salvaggio M V L116 fb 8.00 72-23 *Service*1162¾ Perplexing116nk *Barley Creek*1161½ Mild rally 8
29May02-9Pen fst 6f :223 :452 :58 1:11 3↑ Clm 7500N1Y 49 5 8 89½ 811 810 613 Hemmings T7 L115 fb 8.30 77-14 Bearcat Ruckus122¾ *Jebular*1163¼ *Hawkwatch*1173¾ Bumped start 8
8May02-7Pen fst 1 :241 :484 1:132 1:401 3↑ Clm c-5000N2Y 67 6 11 11 1½ 1½ 11¼ Nieto C L122 fb 3.80 84-20 Miles River1221¼ Tibet1196 Conniving Sal119nk Rail 2nd, driving 7
Claimed from Castro Rafael for $5,000, Castro Rafael Trainer 2002(as of 05/08): (7 2 0 0 0.29)
26Apr02-3Pen fst 5½f :222 :462 :584 1:05 3↑ Clm 5000N1Y 65 2 6 42 52½ 31½ 1nk Nieto C L122 fb 7.00 91-13 *Miles River*122nk Grinanbearit122nk Prospect Heights1191½ 2 wide, driving 7
WORKS: Oct18 Pen 4f fst :491 H *3/22* Sep19 Pen 5f fst 1:022 H *1/2*
TRAINER: Dirt(172 .13 $1.67) Routes(80 .15 $1.89) Claim(153 .12 $1.33)

Rhythm Band
Own: al Maktoum Mohammed b
Gr/ro h. 6
Sire: Cozzene (Caro*Ire) $60,000
Dam: Golden Wave Band(Dixieland Band)
Br: Clifton William L Jr (Ky)
Tr: McLaughlin Kiaran P (—) 2002:(98 26 .27)

Life	18	5	2	2	$1,349,372	99	D.Fst	1	0	0	0	$0 –
2002	9	2	1	0	$71,565	99	Wet(325)	0	0	0	0	$0 –
2001	1	0	0	1	$3,268	–	Turf(335)	17	5	2	2	$1,349,372 99
CSC	0	0	0	0	$0	–	Dist	0	0	0	0	$0 –

22Sep02-5Bel fm 1 Ⓣ :22 :441 1:082 1:331 4↑ Clm 100000(100-75) **99** 4 77½ 85¾ 31 13 14¼ Migliore R L121 *1.60e 94-07 Rhythm Band1214¼ Zoning116hd *Silver Rail*1181¼ Inside move, driving 9
6Sep02-7Bel gd 1 Ⓣ :23 :46 1:093 1:34 3↑ Alw 58000C **91** 9 72½ 75½ 61½ 86 75½ Migliore R L122 7.50 84-14 Baptize1202 *Green Fee*120hd Sardaukar122nk No response 9
10Aug02-9Sar fm 1½ 🅃 :471 1:113 2:002 2:24 3↑ SwordDancrH-G1 **65** 8 98½ 71¾ 1111 1122 1124½ Migliore R L114 36.75 88-06 *With Anticipation*120hd *Denon*1181¾ Volponi115nk Steadied after start 11
17Jly02-5Bel fm 1⅛ 🅃 :491 1:121 1:36 1:481 4↑ Alw 50000N3X **98** 1 52½ 51½ 51¾ 31½ 11¼ Migliore R L119f *1.30 88-20 RhythmBnd1191¼ SpottdOwl121nk RlctntGroom1161 3 wide move, driving 6
22Jun02-9Mth fm 1 Ⓣ :231 :464 1:102 1:344 3↑ OClm 50000(50-45)N **95** 2 52¼ 53½ 63¼ 53 2nk Velez J A Jr L118f *1.50 95-06 *Autonomy*121nk *Rhythm Band*1181¾ Spruce Run1181 Closed gamely 8
16May02-8Bel fm 1⅜ 🅃 :474 1:122 1:362 2:131 4↑ Alw 50000N3X **91** 4 11½ 16 2hd 21 63½ Migliore R L117f 4.30 83-19 DeputyStrike1211¼ SovereignKit112½ PerfectStrnger117nk Set pace, tired 8
Previously trained by Sateesh Seemar
15Mar02 ♦ Jebel Ali(UAE) fst *1 RH 1:373 4↑ Jebel Ali Mile (Listed) 916¼ Durcan T E 123 – Pacino1233½ Zoning123¾ Man Howa1231½ 10
Timeform rating: 77 Stk 95300 *Rated in 6th,weakened 2f out.Jila 4th*
2Mar02 ♦ NadAlSheba(UAE) gd *1⅛ Ⓣ LH 1:52 3↑ Jebel Hatta-G3 41¾ Birrer G 126 – Divine Task1261 Lightning Arrow126½ Superiority126nk 10
Timeform rating: 111 Stk 95300 *Rated in 5th,3rd 3f out,one-paced final furlong.Summoner 6th*
24Feb02 ♦ NadAlSheba(UAE) gd *1½ Ⓣ LH 2:323 4↑ Dubai City of Gold-G3 714½ Birrer G 121 – Narrative1193¼ Grandera1193¼ Celtic Silence1191¼ 7
Timeform rating: 95 Stk 95300 *Towards rear throughout.Musha Merr 5th.No betting*
8Apr01 ♦ Abu Dhabi(UAE) gd *1⅜ Ⓣ RH 2:153 3↑ Abu Dhabi Championship 32 Birrer G 129 – Alva Glen127½ Inchlonaig1261½ Rhythm Band129¾ 7
Timeform rating: 111 Alw 32600 *Rated in 5th,mild bid over 1f out,no late response*
WORKS: Dec1 **GP** 5f fst 1:012 B *3/8* Nov24 **GP** 4f fst :494 B *8/10*

The symmetry of Runspastum's form is remarkable. If you anticipated further improvement from him in the Iselin on August 18, you had a very live 37-1 shot. Misspent completed an almost equally perfect cycle on August 9, winning at 5-1. On August 1 at Saratoga, This Guns For Hire was a very solid 5-2 winner. Rhythm Band was even more solid on September 22 as the 8-5 favorite. Finally, Miles River cycled up to a 74 to win by 1¾ lengths at 8-1 on November 3.

A careful look at the 2-year-old filly Concerta provides a textbook case of how projecting improvement in Beyer figures can bring big value.

10 Concerta
Own:Kitos Belinda M
Royal Blue White Cross Of Lorraine
$16,000
RIVERA J A II (11 1 2 2 .09) 2002:(478 42 .09)
B. f. 2 (Jan)
Sire: Concerto (Chief's Crown) $3,500
Dam: Greek Code(Probable)
Br: Belinda M Kitos & Dr Robert J Kitos (Fla)
Tr: Delk Danny(2 0 1 0 .00) 2002:(118 13 .11)
L 119

Life	11	2	1	1	$25,540	62	D.Fst	8	1	1	0	$13,170 62
2002	11	2	1	1	$25,540	62	Wet(304)	3	1	0	1	$12,370 52
2001	0	M	0	0	$0	–	Turf(251)	0	0	0	0	$0 –
Crc	11	2	1	1	$25,540	62	Dst(259)	4	1	1	1	$12,620 62

24Oct02-4Crc fst 5½f :222 :47 1:002 1:072 ⒻClm 16000(16-14)N2L **62** 4 1 2hd 11½ 11 11½ Rivera J A II L118b 15.00 85-16 Concerta1181½ She's Cooking Now1185 Lucky Fab1181¼ Off rail, prevailed 6
6Oct02-9Crc fst 7f :22 :453 1:122 1:27 ⒻClm 22500(25-22.5)N2L **41** 7 3 31 33½ 55¾ 510 Rivera J A II L116b 41.20 69-16 DinnerSweets1184½ Denimsnddimonds118hd PstFzool1184¾ 3 wide, faltered 7
7Sep02-11Crc fst 5f :214 :461 :593 ⒻClm 22500(25-22.5) **27** 1 1 54½ 78 910 914¼ Rivera J A II L114b 22.50 77-15 SuprBrbr1112¼ ElctrclCrlt1153¼ Dnmsnddmonds118½ Saved ground, faded 9
20Aug02-7Crc fst 6f :221 :46 :591 1:132 ⒻClm 20000(20-18) **40** 2 4 2hd 1hd 22½ 47 Rivera J A II L118b 3.90 70-11 RedMoonRising1155¼ JolieGood1151½ WildBlubrry115hd Slow st, vied, tired 6
11Aug02-10Crc sly 4½f :23 :472 :54 ⒻMd 20000(20-18) **52** 4 1 13 14 14¼ Rivera J A II L118b *2.00 89-11 Concerta1184¼ *La Roverina*118¾ Keep It Comin1163¾ Inside, driving 10
19Jly02-3Crc fst 4½f :223 :471 :534 ⒻMd 25000(25-22.5) **38** 5 5 65¼ 56 46¼ Cruz M R 118b 2.50 84-10 AnswerTheStorm1181 LndTheLimit1184 EndlssPlsur1181¼ Lacked a rally 7
8Jly02-6Crc sly 5f :223 :474 1:013 ⒻMd 25000(25-22.5) **43** 7 2 31 2hd 3½ 31¾ Bain G W 118b 3.00e 79-17 **Coppergoldn'silver**1181¾ Luck Liz118no Concerta118½ 3 wide, missed 2nd 7
28Jun02-6Crc fst 5f :224 :472 1:002 ⒻMd 30000(32-30) **49** 4 1 1½ 11 2hd 22 Bain G W 116b 12.80 85-10 **Laura Lynn**1182 Concerta1161¾ Lady Helma1184 Inside, outfinished 6
15Jun02-4Crc sly 4½f :233 :481 :543 ⒻMd 30000(32-30) **43** 6 4 2½ 43 44½ Camejo O5 111 11.20 81-16 Where Are You116nk Super Barbara1182¾ ***Laura Lynn***1181½ 3 wide, tired 7
7Jun02-6Crc fst 4½f :224 :472 :54 ⒻMd 25000(25-22.5) **29** 5 7 58 58½ 410¼ Camejo O5 113 9.60 79-12 **ArtfulLdy**118½ TouchLightly1186¾ Ndnointroduction1183 Stumbled start 7
WORKS: Oct18 **Crc** 5f fst 1:023 B *4/23* Sep22 **Crc** 5f fst 1:013 H *2/13* ● Aug4 **Crc** 3f fst :354 H *1/20*
TRAINER: 2YO(48 .04 $0.79) Dirt(119 .10 $1.33) Sprint(99 .10 $1.40) Claim(50 .20 $2.65)

In the fourth race at Calder on October 24 there were five fillies that had recently run figures in the low-to-mid 50's. At first glance the race looked too difficult, the runners too evenly matched. But the pattern of Concerta's figures brought order—and value—out of seeming chaos.

- She's Cooking Now had recent Beyers of 54-44-50-57-52. She looked pretty solid at this level.
- Lucky Fab had run figures of 57 and 51 before being stretched out to a mile, where she ran a dismal 31. Now she was being dropped slightly and turned back to $5^{1}/_{2}$ furlongs. She certainly had to be considered.
- Majorannouncement had figures of 55 and 49 at Finger Lakes, but had most recently been shipped to Belmont for a New York-bred stakes race. She was eased at seven furlongs. Beyer: below zero. You couldn't tell what she might do at Calder.
- Seaventure had run Beyers of 61-56-51 in May and June at a much higher level, but she had been struggling ever since. Her Beyers had declined to 23-46-41. With no recent improvement, this signaled a very negative pattern. And she had now been laid off for seven weeks and was dropping again in class. All signs were negative.
- Concerta showed a consistent, repetitive pattern of cycling Beyers. Back in June she had run 29-43-49. Then she had improved again up to a 52 in August, although that number was earned on a sloppy track. Now she had put together figures of 27 and 41. She had earned the most recent number at a slightly higher level and at seven furlongs, a distance that was probably well beyond her best but could give her more stamina on the turn-back to $5^{1}/_{2}$.

Because Concerta's very competitive Beyer of 52 was run in August, the bettors neglected her. She went to the post at odds of 15-1, even though she had at least as good a chance as anyone else in this field. She won fairly easily, and paid $32. The most logical horses, She's Cooking Now and Lucky Fab, finished second and third. Exacta: $121.20. Trifecta: $266.60. That's how a dynamic view of the Beyer Speed Figures can bring special value.

A slight variation on this cycling theme—the interrupted cycle—is clearly illustrated by the past performances of River Spirit.

7 River Spirit
Own:Broman Chester & Mary R
Green And White Diagonal Quarters, White
SANTOS J A (68 10 6 9 .15) 2002:(1075 165 .15)

Gr/ro g. 4 (Apr)
Sire: Silver Ghost (Mr. Prospector) $15,000
Dam: River Sunrise(Riverman)
Br: Chester Broman & Mary R Broman (NY)
Tr: Hernandez Ramon M(5 0 1 0 .00) 2002:(122 15 .12)

L 120

Life	24	4	1	3	$116,610	91	D.Fst	19	3	1	2	$98,680	86
2002	12	3	1	0	$63,970	91	Wet(320)	4	1	0	1	$17,930	91
2001	7	0	0	3	$16,940	78	Turf(305)	1	0	0	0	$0	60
Aqu	4	0	0	0	$2,640	72	Dst(320)	7	2	0	0	$50,880	91

17Oct02-1Bel	gd	1		:231	:462	1:11	1:354	3↑ Clm 20000 (20-18)	91	2	87½	87	42	1½	14¼	Santos J A	L 117 fb	8.00	90-15 River Spirit1174¼ Boeing1201¾ Warm April1203¼ 5 wide move, driving 8
25Sep02-9Bel	fm	1⅛	Ⓣ	:48	1:12	1:362	1:482	3↑ ⓈAlw 48000N2X	60	10	109½	1014	1016	1016	911½	Santos J A	L 121 fb	16.70	75-14 Robbie's Rockin117½ Saf Link121nk Stogie Two1211¾ No factor 10
26Aug02-2Sar	fst	1⅛		:491	1:133	1:39	1:521	3↑ ⓈAlw 46000N2X	71	2	66	51¾	42	54	59	Santos J A	L 121 fb	7.60	69-25 RunningTody121½ SeekingThMony1175 Aspirin121¾ 4 wide move, faded 6
7Aug02-4Sar	fst	1⅛		:481	1:124	1:381	1:513	3↑ ⓈAlw 46000N2X	63	5	68½	610	68	511	616½	Santos J A	L 122 fb	4.60	64-20 PrivtePrctice1183¼ *RunningTody*1203½ Thebigppl1164½ 4 wide trip, nothing 6
5Jly02-4Bel	fst	1		:23	:454	1:104	1:361	3↑ ⓈAlw 44000N1X	86	8	86	710	33½	1½	14½	Santos J A	L 122 fb	13.50	88-18 RiverSpirit1224½ Thermopylae1223½ **QuatreDixNeuf**1171½ 4 wide, ridden out 8
16Jun02-9Bel	fst	7f		:223	:453	1:10	1:231	4↑ Clm 22500 (25-20)	73	4	7	96¾	95	56½	56½	Villafan R	L 115 fb	36.50	80-10 *GrnRichs*1201¾ Who'sTlking1201¾ Whitwtrspritzr1201½ Inside trip, no rally 9
11May02-1Bel	fst	1⅛		:48	1:132	1:39	1:514	4↑ Clm 25000 (25-20)	44	7	64¼	62½	2½	920	929½	Villafan R5	L 112 fb	21.40	41-29 DrwngAwy1206½ CzrdsDncr1204¼ CorprtPhn1201¼ Stumbled start, bumped 9
20Apr02-7Aqu	sly	1	⊗	:231	:46	1:11	1:373	3↑ ⓈAlw 44000N1X	58	5	610	413	45	57½	67	Villafan R5	L 117 fb	*1.75	71-16 Bigwinedrinker122hd Gave Away1242¼ Iolite1221¼ Wide, no response 9
9Mar02-9Aqu	fst	1 1/16	⊡	:232	:473	1:121	1:46	4↑ ⓈAlw 44000N1X	70	8	710	78	54½	1hd	2hd	Villafan R5	L 113 fb	3.60	76-19 Anties Boy120hd River Spirit1134¼ River Course1181¼ 5 wide move, gamely 9
16Feb02-9Aqu	fst	1⅛	⊡	:491	1:134	1:394	1:531	4↑ Clm 25000N2L	73	2	31	42	32½	17	17½	Villafan R5	L 110 fb	8.70	71-19 RiverSpirit1107½ CarpeDemon118nk PeakAffir120¾ Drew away under drive 8
20Jan02-5Aqu	fst	1 1/16	⊡	:23	:472	1:13	1:462	4↑ ⓈAlw 44000N1X	40	8	42	42½	52	813	821	Lezcano L5	L 113 fb	5.50	53-24 MricopCounty1183½ HopToProspr1181½ AntsBoy1205 Chased 4 wide, tired 9
6Jan02-5Aqu	fst	1 1/16	⊡	:234	:49	1:141	1:454	4↑ ⓈAlw 44000N1X	68	10	86	104	106¾	88¾	45	Lezcano L5	L 112 fb	10.40	72-21 J S Mosby117hd *Maricopa County*1172¾ AntiesBoy1222¼ Going well outside 11

WORKS: Oct9 Bel tr.t 4f fst :501 B *10/18* Sep19 Bel tr.t 4f fst :491 B *12/34* Sep13 Bel tr.t 5f fst 1:04 B *4/5* Sep4 Bel tr.t 4f fst :51 B *11/14* Aug23 Sar tr.t 5f fst 1:063 B *6/6* Aug18 Sar tr.t 5f fst 1:054 B *37/41*
TRAINER: Dirt(216 .13 $1.75) Alw(105 .10 $1.30)

The favorite in the first race at Belmont Park on October 17 was Warm April. He had been dropping steadily since he ran figures in the mid-90's in California in the spring, at that point competing with $40,000 claimers and allowance company. But he had just run back-to-back Beyers of 83 and 85, winning his previous race, a seven-furlong sprint at the $16,000 level. With this apparently good recent form Warm April went off at even money.

But River Spirit caught my eye immediately. Back on July 5 he had run a powerful race with a Beyer of 86, at the mile distance, around one turn—the same conditions that he would face on October 17. He had won basically in hand after a big four-wide move. But he didn't fare nearly as well around two turns at Saratoga. On August 7 he was four-wide on both turns, trailing the field behind a slow pace. The winner of that race went wire to wire, and the first two finishers raced on the rail. River Spirit bounced down to a 63. He improved somewhat next time out, earning a Beyer of 71. Once again he raced very wide while the first two finishers came up the rail. Then, after a one-month layoff, trainer Mike Hernandez put him on the turf, which he apparently hated. Now, on October 17, if he could continue his cycle back up to an 86 or thereabouts—a cycle interrupted by the grass race—he would be at least as strong a play as Warm April.

And he wasn't overbet at even money. Because his best race was buried four races back, River Spirit went off at 8-1.

River Spirit trailed in the early going and, as usual, moved very wide around the entire field. He drew off strongly and won by $4^{1}/4$ lengths. He paid $18 and ran a Beyer figure of 91, cycling even beyond his earlier 86. The heavily favored Warm April chased the pace on the outside on the turn, didn't respond when asked, and was well beaten.

The grass race provided a brief interruption in River Spirit's progress. With other horses it could be a terrible trip or an extremely biased track or a sloppy surface—some big excuse for a disappointing effort. When you find such a situation, it's worth looking into it a lot more deeply, as River Spirit demonstrates.

Before we go any farther, a warning needs to be issued here: It's one thing to identify horses in a possible cycling pattern. It's quite another thing to decide that you should bet on them. Nothing should be accepted uncritically in this game, and cycling horses should not be considered, in any sense, "automatic" bets. Identifying a cycling pattern does not mean that you can forget about other elements of handicapping. It should be a key supplement to your handicapping, not a substitute for broad, multifaceted analysis.

For example, a horse named Groovy Minister had run a 65 Beyer when loose on the lead on September 14 at Pimlico. Then he bounced down to a 28 and subsequently improved to a 56 at Pimlico on October 22. Would he now, on November 5, cycle all the way back to a 65 or beyond? At even money, it was an important question. The circumstances of the race said that Groovy Minister would not be able to improve further. He had the outside post in an eight-horse field around two turns at Delaware, a distinct disadvantage. He had earned that earlier 65 when loose on the lead. But today it didn't look like he would ever be able to get the lead. He was, in short, up against it, both in terms of pace and position.

As could have been anticipated, on November 5 Groovy

Minister was hung four- and five-wide on the first turn, tried to move up to chase on the backstretch, but couldn't keep up after that impossible trip.

There are dozens of other cases like this. Here are just a few:

- Ibelieveitsours. October 7, Delaware, race 2. She ran a 53 on August 12, followed by a 40 and a 48. But she had two serious drawbacks: After a strong effort she was taking a sharp drop; and that previous hard effort had come at a mile—a potentially draining race for a cheap filly who had previously been sprinting. On the turn-back to six furlongs she ran fifth with only a 37 Beyer.

- Hunka Hunka Lori Z. October 8, Laurel, race 6. She had a big back figure of 87. Since that race she had declined to a 79 and a 59, then improved again to a 76. Her most recent race at Timonium was absolutely horrible (she was eased with a Beyer of 22). Perhaps she just couldn't handle the Timonium bull ring. Perhaps she could continue cycling back to that 87. There was only one problem: That 87 had occurred a long time before, on May 1—more than five months in the past. That's well beyond the statute of limitations for figure cycling. On October 8 she never even approached that 87. She ran only a 67.

- I've Got My Sox On. September 24, Philadelphia, race 4. She had run a 54 on May 30 at Penn National, followed by 43-39-50. Her apparent cycle was interrupted in her last start by a two-turn race, in a higher class, on a sloppy track—certainly an excusable effort. But I could see a few serious warning signs:
    1. She was an 8-year-old mare with only 47 lifetime starts.
    2. She had run that 2002-best of 54 nearly four months ago.
    3. She had not raced for more than five weeks—seldom a good sign with such a low-level claimer.

On September 24 she finished a distant fourth with a figure of 35.

- Dont Run Getthegun. September 17, Philadelphia, race 6. This mare is a two-turn specialist. Her big Beyer of 62 was earned while loose on the lead at one mile and 70 yards. Following Beyers of 39 and 51, she was now being dropped for the second consecutive time and turned back to a one-turn race at seven furlongs. In addition, she would be facing two other high-speed sprinters. She was up against it in a big way, as the race on September 17 showed. She ran third with only a 52 Beyer.

- Brightest Ice. September 29, Belmont, race 1. This 3-year-old gelding was an interesting case. He had cycled from 52 to 72 to 81, then down to 42, up to 73, and now looked like a perfect candidate to return to the low 80's. Well, almost perfect. The only problem was a recent drop in class from consistent races at $50,000 down to $25,000. Perhaps there was nothing physically wrong. Since Brightest Ice had only won one race in his life—more than a year ago in September 2001—it could be that his connections were sick and tired of watching him lose. Still, the drop in class raised some doubt, as did the fact that his 81 Beyer had been earned while setting an uncontested pace and tiring to finish third. On September 29, Brightest Ice improved a bit, up to a Beyer of 76, but it was only good enough for third place.

All these examples show how every judgment about speed-figure patterns must be evaluated in context—taking into account all the traditional elements of class, trainers, distance, recency, and trips. By way of contrast with all the above flawed examples, here's a more pristine case, that of Nasty Storm in the Gallant Bloom Handicap at Belmont Park.

1 Nasty Storm
Own:Stronach Stable
Black, Gold Ball, Two Red
DOUGLAS R R (—) 2002:(1166 228 .20)

Ch. f. 4 (Apr)
Sire: Gulch (Mr. Prospector) $50,000
Dam: A Stark Is Born(Graustark)
Br: Grousemont Farm (Ky)
Tr: Stewart Dallas (—) 2002:(361 40 .11)

L 116

Life	22	8	3	3	$737,657	102
2002	7	2	0	1	$150,804	100
2001	8	5	0	1	$383,338	102
Aqu	0	0	0	0	$0	–
D.Fst	19	8	2	3	$693,017	102
Wet(345)	2	0	1	0	$44,640	79
Turf(285)	1	0	0	0	$0	74
Dst(320)	1	1	0	0	$137,764	101

6Oct02-8Bel	fst	6½f	$:22^2$	$:45^2$	$1:10^4$	$1:17^4$	3↑	ⒻGallantBlmH-G2	100	6	2	$3^{1\frac{1}{2}}$	$3^{\frac{1}{2}}$	1^{hd}	1^1	Santos J A	L 114 b	14.40	86–19	NastyStorm114¹ RagingFever120¾ *ShineAgin*118⁴½	Speed 3 wide, driving	6
7Sep02-9TP	fst	6f	$:21^3$	$:44^3$	$:57^2$	$1:10^2$	3↑	ⒻWkendDelight75k	91	2	5	4^2	$4^{1\frac{1}{2}}$	4^2	$3^{3\frac{1}{2}}$	Court J K	L 113 b	*1.80	87–22	Don'tCountessOut113³ SilentStream113nk *NstyStorm*113⁵½	Boxed in turn	9
25Aug02-9Sar	fst	7f	$:21^4$	$:44$	$1:08^4$	$1:22^1$	3↑	ⒻBallerina H-G1	74	7	3	$6^{1\frac{3}{4}}$	6^6	5^{11}	5^{14}	Day P	L 115 b	13.40	80–06	ShineAgain116½ RagingFever121¼ ***Mandy'sGold***118¹⁰	4 wide, no response	7
2Aug02-8Sar	sly	6f	$:22$	$:44^4$	$:56^3$	$1:09^1$	3↑	ⒻHonrblMissH-G3	79	6	3	2^{hd}	$4^{\frac{3}{4}}$	$5^{6\frac{1}{2}}$	6^{11}	Day P	L 116 b	5.30	85–21	**Mndy'sGold**116¹¾ *ShinAgin*116³ *DtYouMizBlu*114¹¼	Chased outside, tired	6
3Jly02-9CD	fst	6f	$:21^4$	$:45$	$:56^4$	$1:09$	3↑	ⒻAlw 56525N$Y	100	3	1	2^1	1^{hd}	$1^{1\frac{1}{2}}$	$1^{3\frac{1}{4}}$	Day P	L 115 b	*.50	93–12	NastyStorm115³¼ DorothyAnn115¾ Hattiesburg115¹¼	Pressed 4w,hand urg	5
4May02-7CD	fst	7f	$:22^3$	$:45^1$	$1:09^4$	$1:22^4$	4↑	ⒻHumanaDstfH-G1	91	9	1	5^2	4^2	4^1	$5^{2\frac{1}{2}}$	Day P	L 117 b	3.00	86–08	[D]Gold Mover115hd CelticMelody114¹¼ Hattiesburg115¹	Lean in bmp 3/16s	9
10Apr02-8Kee	fst	7f	$:22^1$	$:45$	$1:10^2$	$1:23^3$	4↑	ⒻMadison111k	94	3	1	2^{hd}	2^{hd}	4^1	$5^{2\frac{3}{4}}$	Day P	L 123 b	2.90	83–15	Victory Ride116¹ *Celtic Melody*116½ Away116¹¼	Forced pace,weakened	7
3Nov01-9CD	fst	1	$:23$	$:46^1$	$1:10^2$	$1:35^1$	3↑	ⒻCD DistaffH-G2	101	6	1^{hd}	$1^{1\frac{1}{2}}$	1^1	$1^{1\frac{1}{2}}$	$1^{1\frac{1}{4}}$	Day P	L 115 b	*1.20	91–14	Nasty Storm115¹¼ *Forest Secrets*113¹ Trip117¹¼	Off inside, driving	8
10Oct01-8Kee	fst	7f	$:22^2$	$:45^1$	$1:10^3$	$1:23^1$		ⒻRaven Run109k	100	2	1	3^{nk}	1^{hd}	1^{hd}	$1^{1\frac{1}{2}}$	Day P	L 123 b	*.80	86–22	*NstyStorm*123¹½ *Httiesburg*123²¼ ForstScrts123⁵¼	Repelled bid,game,drvg	7
15Sep01-13TP	fst	6f	$:21^4$	$:44^4$	$:57^1$	$1:09^4$	3↑	ⒻWkendDelight75k	102	2	4	2^2	$2^{1\frac{1}{2}}$	2^1	1^1	Court J K	L 116 b	2.10	92–17	*Nasty Storm*116¹ Hidden Assets113³¼ City Fair116½	Off inside, driving	6
28Jly01-8Sar	fst	7f	$:21^2$	$:44$	$1:08^4$	$1:21^3$		ⒻTest-G1	93	6	8	8^{18}	7^{10}	$4^{4\frac{1}{2}}$	$3^{6\frac{1}{4}}$	Day P	L 120 b	9.10	91–06	*Victory Ride*116³¼ *Xtra Heat*123³ *Nasty Storm*120nk	Unprepared for start	8
16Jun01-10CD	gd	$1\frac{1}{16}$ Ⓣ	$:24$	$:47^4$	$1:12^1$	$1:42^3$		ⒻRegret-G3	74	1	2^{hd}	1^1	$2^{\frac{1}{2}}$	7^8	$8^{9\frac{3}{4}}$	Meche L J	L 117 b	7.60	83–07	Casual Feat115¹ Amaretta117¹¼ La Vida Loca119¹½	Bmp start,faded inside	8

WORKS: Nov25 CD 4f fst $:47^4$ B *3/25* Nov19 CD 6f fst $1:15^4$ B *6/7* Nov11 CD 5f fst $1:01^3$ B *14/37* Sep29 CD 4f fst $:50^2$ B *27/35* Sep18 CD 4f fst $:48^2$ B *3/40* Sep2 Sar 4f fst :49 B *11/41*
TRAINER: Sprint/Route(84 .07 $0.85) 31-60Days(196 .10 $0.95) Dirt(603 .12 $1.20) GrdStk(50 .08 $1.51)

After her September 7 race Nasty Storm appeared headed toward another triple-digit Beyer, and, in a compact six-horse field, only two of them—Raging Fever and Shine Again—provided any real competition at that level of Beyer figures. Nasty Storm went off at odds of 14-1, and closed to win by a length. Raging Fever filled out the exacta.

Finally, remember Glamdring? The seemingly ugly dog at the beginning of this chapter? Now you should be able to see the merits of his superficially poor past performances.

On August 10, after a four-month layoff, Glamdring had been banged around at the start, angled out very wide at the top of the stretch, and failed to make any serious progress against a field of killers—although he did persevere to finish fourth. The winner of that race, Warners, ran a huge Beyer of 109, so Glamdring, despite finishing $9\frac{1}{2}$ lengths behind, still earned a strong figure of 85. In his next race Glamdring ran very poorly, managing a Beyer of only 59. Then he showed significant improvement in his next start, despite the fact that he was racing on a very muddy track and he was rushed off his feet while uncharacteristically chasing the pace.

On October 23 Glamdring was entered in a high-priced claimer at Aqueduct—a much softer field than he had been facing. The race was full of speed, so if he returned to his normal closer's style he would very likely benefit from the way the race would be run. In addition, there were only one or two other strong contenders in this seven-horse field, and if he could cycle back up to a figure in the upper 80's he would be a very serious factor. He was no cinch, but only someone with an eye trained on his Beyer Speed Figure pattern would have focused on him as the key to value.

The race set up perfectly for Glamdring, with three horses battling for the lead on the front end. Glamdring sat a few lengths behind them and then roared through the stretch to win by two lengths. He exploded to a figure of 97. You certainly couldn't have predicted that kind of improvement. But, if you didn't penetrate the pattern of his Beyers, you might well have dismissed him as a hopeless case.

The point, again, is simple: A dynamic approach to the Beyer Speed Figures—in this case projecting improvement—can be the key to value. And value is what this game is all about.

BEYERS ON GRASS

EVERYONE SEEMS TO agree: Turf figures are a problem. Some would say "problematical" might capture it more accurately. Others might say that grass figures are a menace, even a curse. But, for better or worse, they have to be calculated and they have to be dealt with.

I approached a number of professional handicappers and speed-figure specialists and their responses ranged from a cautious distancing from the entire question of grass figures, to disclaimers about their reliability, to distaste and even disgust with the whole issue. One extremist dismissed all turf figures as useless concoctions, and called for the abolition of all grass racing as the only foolproof way to eliminate the problem of turf figures once and for all.

"I hate turf figures," said handicapping author Tom Brohamer. "They're only as good as the person doing them."

Maury Wolff, an expert handicapper, was equally blunt: "Miss Cleo considers them to be a valuable tool," he said—a not very subtle relegation of turf figures to the realm of the charlatan, the mystic, and the occult.

If you're going to write about turf figures, Andrew Beyer advised me, "Honesty is the best policy." In other words, we have to produce them. We do the very best we can. They're as accurate as we can make them. But they simply can't be as reliable as dirt figures. It's not in their nature.

No matter where speed-figure analysts come down on the utility of turf figures, they all seem to agree on one thing: Grass figures and grass racing are profoundly different from dirt figures and dirt racing. The reasons?

First, solid dirt figures are derived from solidly based track variants, which in turn are dependent on adequate samples and accurate timings. Since we seldom have a sufficient sample of grass races on any given day, and the timings are rather iffy, no reliable variant can be made. Turf figures just can never overcome that crippling reality: a lack of sufficient reliable data.

Second, the essential contours of turf courses can change from day to day as the false rails are moved in and out in order to prevent the grass from getting completely chopped to pieces. And so timings and distances lack the precision we're accustomed to on the dirt.

Third, the pace scenarios are different, with early speed being less of a factor. Many experts are convinced that late fractions are much more significant, even decisive, in grass racing.

Fourth, the figure patterns of turf horses generally are more consistent than those of dirt horses. Big bounces are less frequent, according to Len Ragozin, and the patterns "less ragged." The figures among contenders in a typical grass race are much more tightly bunched. This greater consistency could result from many factors: Turf horses run less frequently, so they are fresher; most grass races are routes, and these horses are generally more consistent, even on the dirt; and grass racing could be less wearing on a horse, particularly with the reduction of stress from the softer footing and the generally less frantic early pace.

Whatever the reasons, most analysts have concluded that grass racing is a species apart.

So, what should we do with the Beyer Speed Figures in turf races? Should we ignore them completely? Treat them with a grain (or more) of salt? Use them simply as "ballpark" guidelines, as a sort of class rating system on the model of the European Timeform ratings?

In order to answer these questions, I decided to go back to basics. I made a study of the performance of the Beyer Speed Figures in grass races, beginning at the beginning. I wanted to know how the top Beyers did in turf races compared to dirt races. A simple inquiry. Unfortunately, the methodology was not so simple. I had to make up some strict rules to follow:

▶ I only considered races where more than half the runners had recent turf form. That eliminated races where most horses had never run on the turf, or hadn't run on the turf in months or even years.

▶ If a horse's most recent race was on the dirt, but he had run on the grass two races back, I accepted that figure as his last-race Beyer.

▶ If the winner of a grass race was a first-time starter, a first-time turfer, or an import with no previous Beyers on the grass, I accepted the second-place finisher as the yardstick to measure the performance of the top figure against the rest of the field.

Obviously I had to make occasional judgments about which races to include and which races to leave out, and I did this in what I believe was a completely unbiased manner. In any case, my purpose was not to arrive at some scientifically precise percentage of top-Beyer winners on the grass. That would have been much too ambitious, considering the many methodological problems involved. Rather, I was looking to get some general indication of how these top-figure horses held up on the turf—to assess their overall value as handicapping tools, particularly as compared to the Beyer figures on dirt.

I began my study in southern California. I analyzed every grass race between the opening of the Santa Anita winter meeting in December 2000 and the end of the Del Mar meeting in September 2002. The results were quite surprising. Out of 876 turf races, 325 were won by the top Beyer grass figure. That's an amazing 37.1 percent. If you exclude ties (that is, co-top Beyers who won), the percentage drops only to 32.5 percent. That's higher than any corresponding dirt study I've ever encountered.

Of course, if grass racing is different, then southern California grass racing could be even more different. Course conditions seldom change, and there are very few shippers from other North American tracks. So perhaps this high percentage could be misleading. More evidence would be needed from other tracks.

Saratoga seemed like a natural counterweight. The turf racing is extremely complicated, with changing weather and grass conditions—and with shippers from all over the United States and beyond. So I analyzed all the grass races from 2000, 2001, and 2002. Out of 232 races on the turf, there were 82 top-Beyer winners—a remarkable 35.3 percent (30.9 percent if ties are excluded).

Still, I was not convinced. After all, southern California and Saratoga represented the classiest racing in America—especially on the grass. So I expanded my study to include the races from Delaware Park, Gulfstream Park, and the Kentucky circuit. Here are the results for 2002:

TRACK	NUMBER OF RACES	TOP-BEYER WINNERS	TIES
Delaware	131	49	7
Gulfstream	82	26	2
Keeneland, Churchill	184	54	7

At Delaware the winning percentage was 37.4 percent (33.9 percent without ties). At Gulfstream Park the winning percentage was 31.7 percent (30 percent without ties). In Kentucky it was 29.3 percent (26.5 percent without ties).

So this study included 1,493 races from eight different tracks. The total of top-Beyer winners was 533 (with 88 co-top figures). That translated to a winning percentage of 35.7 percent (31.7 percent without ties). At every track studied, the winning percentage for top Beyer figures on the grass was at least as high, and in most cases substantially higher, than any comparable study of Beyer figures on the dirt.

What does it all mean? Certainly no one could dispute the fact that grass racing is indeed different. But few writers and handicappers have considered that some of those very differences might encourage greater reliability in turf figures and help to explain the surprisingly strong performance of top Beyers on the grass:

- Nearly all grass races are distance races. There are many fewer stretch-outs or turn-backs, or drastic changes in distance for the great majority of horses. Turf sprinters at tracks such as Monmouth, Delaware, or Laurel tend to specialize in those races, and two-turn turfers rarely turn back to five-furlong grass races. So there is a greater consistency than with dirt races.

- Turf races are more widely spaced. Because turf racing is very much secondary at most tracks and turf races are much less frequently carded, most turf horses have longer respites between races. That could be another factor encouraging greater consistency of performance.

- Most tracks (especially the more elite venues) do not run grass races below a certain very high level. For example, in New York there are no grass races for maiden claimers or for claiming horses below $35,000. So when you study grass races, you are by definition studying a higher-quality subset of the total Thoroughbred population.

All these factors help to explain the greater consistency of grass runners—which might, in turn, help explain the high percentage of top-Beyer winners. But that very consistency could also work *against* those top-Beyer winners in a number of ways:

- There are many fewer huge gaps in the Beyer figures among turf runners in any particular race—and so there are many fewer big layover numbers compared to dirt races. You rarely see a 1-5 or 2-5 shot on the grass.
- In a typical grass race, the Beyer figures are much more closely clustered. So the slightest change in post position, or trip, or turf condition can easily scramble the results. This was borne out in my analysis of turf races, where a very high proportion of second-top Beyers won on the grass—many of them only one point behind the top figure. And there were many more co-top Beyer winners than on the dirt, as you would expect when the figures are so much more evenly matched.
- A much higher proportion of grass races are run around two tighter turns and have larger fields than the typical dirt race. So there is a much greater opportunity for ground loss and trouble and jockey error—leading to a much greater chance that the fastest horse will not win.

Grass racing is indeed different. Some of those differences work to encourage a higher percentage of top-Beyer winners, and some work against it. But, regardless of these differences, if the statistics presented in this chapter have any validity, then the conclusion is inescapable: The doubts about the value of Beyer Speed Figures in handicapping grass races have been seriously exaggerated.

In turf racing it is probably true that, because of the greater consistency of the horses' Beyer figures on grass, the category of repeat performers is much more prominent. It is also probably true that cycling figure patterns in turf races are not as frequent or as dramatic. And it is also probably true that horses don't bounce as often or as badly on the grass as they do on the dirt.

But it is *not* true that all this renders final-time figures useless or obsolete. If the study of turf races in this chapter is at all a reflection of reality, then the Beyers on grass are at least as reliable as the Beyers on dirt—and they should be used accordingly. And with confidence.

THINKING BEYER

*I*N EVERY RACE you handicap, the infinite combination of variables will inevitably throw up something new and different. So, in writing about handicapping, you can't possibly hope to be "comprehensive," or cover every conceivable circumstance that might arise. That's why learning to "think Beyer" is the most valuable skill you can master—becoming familiar with the best analytical uses of the Beyer Speed Figures so that you can adjust to any set of circumstances you might encounter.

That's what this chapter tries to do. It presents a variety of examples that explore the patterns to be recognized and the pitfalls to be avoided, the plays that offer value and the plays that might be poison. There are bouncers, and horses that refused to bounce. There are successful cyclers, and cyclers that went bust. There are positive patterns and negative patterns. Horses ready to run big races, and horses set to implode. In short, the whole wide range of Beyer Speed Figure scenarios. Or at least a broad suggestion of them.

Big Score		Dk. b or br f. 2 (Mar) FTKJUL01 $72,000		Life	4	3	0	0	$102,965	80	D.Fst	3	3	0	0	$98,465	80
Own: Grunwald Jack		Sire: Grand Slam (Gone West) $25,000		2002	4	3	0	0	$102,965	80	Wet(325)	1	0	0	0	$4,500	22
		Dam: Voluptuous(Cozzene)		2001	0	M	0	0	$0	–	Turf(286)	0	0	0	0	$0	–
		Br: Woodlynn Farm Inc (Ky)		CSC	0	0	0	0	$0	–	Dist	1	1	0	0	$25,265	80
		Tr: Asmussen Steven M (—) 2002:(1809 406 .22)															

13Oct02–8Bel sly 6½f	:21⁴ :45¹ 1:10⁴ 1:17³	Ⓕ Astarita-G2	22 6 4	53¾ 2½ 5¹² 526½	Velazquez J R	L 117 f	4.00	60 – 12 HumorousLdy117ⁿᵒ FstCooki117¹ Chimichurri1174¾			Bumped start, 4 wide	7
14Sep02–9Pha fst 6f	:21³ :44⁴ :57⁴ 1:11¹	Ⓕ Kindergarten75k	74 5 2	2½ 1¹ 1³ 1⁸	Meche D J	L 120 f	*.20	83 – 22 BigScore120⁸ Eliza'sCat114⁶ Mnny'sGoldMker1203½			Drew off, ridden out	5
22Aug02–8Sar fst 6f	:22 :46³ :59² 1:13	Ⓕ Alw 47000n1x	71 1 3	1½ 1½ 11½ 15½ 1¼	Bailey J D	L 119 f	*.95	77 – 20 Big Score119¼ Shesasmokin116ʰᵈ Behrnik116⁵¾			Pace, clear, held on	6
2Jun02–2CD fst 4½f	:21⁴ :45 :51	Ⓕ Md Sp Wt 40k	80 7 5	2ʰᵈ 1³ 1⁶	Meche D J	L 117 f	4.50	100 – 08 BgScor117⁶ WhtsUpPussyct117¹ ChorusGrl1172¾			Bmp start, hand urging	8

"Figs don't lie!" Or so Andrew Beyer is fond of saying, and he's right. But that doesn't mean they aren't subject to endless interpretation, as are all other factors in Thoroughbred handicapping. So there needs to be a corollary to Beyer's confident assertion, and that is, "Trust the figs!" If you're going to use the Beyer Speed Figures in your handicapping, you have to believe that they are an accurate representation of how fast a horse ran in any particular race, and your handicapping has to reflect that conviction.

That's where the example of Big Score comes in. She was entered on October 13 in the Astarita at Belmont Park. Superficially she had many positives: She was a stakes winner, she was undefeated in three starts, and she was trained by a highly successful, high-percentage trainer. She had won her previous race by eight lengths, and it appeared that she probably could have run even faster if asked. For all these reasons she was steadily bet, finally closing at 4-1.

But her Beyer figures could in no way justify such support. Her previous-race figure was actually the lowest of any horse in the field. That 74 Beyer on September 14 represented only a very slight improvement over her 71 on August 22. Perhaps she could have run somewhat faster if she had been in an all-out drive. Perhaps. But even an increase of a few points in her figure would not really have put her in the Astarita mix. And that field she had defeated in Philadelphia was extremely weak. Running in the Astarita was a big step up in class. Nearly all her competition had earned Beyers in the 80's, and against much stronger runners.

In addition, her wire-to-wire win at Saratoga in August had come on a speed-favoring surface. Any objective Beyer-based analysis had to conclude that, despite her superficial appeal, she had absolutely no shot in the Astarita.

Still, despite all this undeniable logic, I had my doubts. Since I'm responsible for producing the Beyer figures for Philadelphia Park, I watched the betting on Big Score and I began to wonder. Perhaps I had made a mistake in calculating her last figure. Should it have been a bit higher? It certainly looked low. Perhaps she had won so easily that, indeed, it was no more than a well-paid workout. And when, in the Astarita, Big Score made a big move on the turn to engage the leaders at the top of the stretch, I really began to worry. Then, in upper stretch, she began to fade, and fade badly. She quickly fell out of contention and retreated far back in the field. She ended up losing by $26\frac{1}{2}$ lengths.

Now, the Belmont track was very sloppy that day, so perhaps Big Score had an excuse for her sudden collapse. But that's not really the point. That 74 in her last race—that's the point. If that represented an accurate measure of her performance that day—and with no indication of any sort of dramatic improvement in the offing—then she should have been 24-1, not 4-1. Whether she ultimately won or lost in the Astarita, a player using speed figures would have had to throw her out. "Figs don't lie," and if you're going to use them, you have to trust them.

---

5 Confess To Me
Own: Bracken Micki
White, Red B, White Cap
BEASLEY J A (82 8 5 11 .10) 2002:(582 58 .10)

B. c. 2 (Feb) KEESEP01 $37,000
Sire: Confide (Phone Trick) $5,000
Dam: Walkerton(Copelan)
Br: Steve C Snowden (Ky)
Tr: Bracken James E(10 3 1 2 .30) 2002:(71 11 .15)

L 117

	Life	3 1 0 0	$12,000	68	D.Fst	3 1 0 0	$12,000	68
	2002	3 1 0 0	$12,000	68	Wet(360)	0 0 0 0	$0	–
	2001	0 M 0 0	$0	–	Turf(243)	0 0 0 0	$0	–
	Crc	3 1 0 0	$12,000	68	Dst(336)	2 1 0 0	$11,800	68

9Nov02– 1Crc fst 6f :22³ :46⁴ :59² 1:12³ Md 50000 (50 -45) 68 6 1 2¹ 2ʰᵈ 1² 17¼ Beasley J A L 120 f 3.70 81–20 Confess To Me120⁷¼ J. R. Belongs120ⁿᵏ Legal Ploy120⁵¼ Drew off, handily 7
26Oct02– 3Crc fst 6f :22¹ :46³ :59² 1:12¹ Md Sp Wt 23k 65 5 5 42½ 62½ 5⁵ 46¾ Beasley J A L 120 21.20 76–17 WhiteBuck120¾ TouchingGold120⁵¼ HesAngel120ⁿᵏ Steadied backstretch 10
28Sep02– 1Crc fst 5f :23 :47⁴ 1:00² Md 50000 (50 -45) 24 1 2 1¹ 1ʰᵈ 43½ 613½ Aguilar M 118 4.10 74–15 Price Of Glory118³¼ CarsonManor118²¾ Snowdazzle118ⁿᵏ Inside, weakened 6
WORKS: Sep14 Crc 4f sly :48⁴ H 2/48 Sep8 Crc 4f sly :49² B (d)4/14 Sep2 Crc 4f fst :49¹ B 7/38
TRAINER: 2YO(33 .24 $1.53) Dirt(152 .18 $1.39) Sprint(124 .17 $1.40) Alw(46 .15 $1.14)

In the first race at Calder on November 9 there was the kind of top figure you could bet with confidence. Not that there wasn't room for surprises. After all, whenever you're dealing with 2-year-old maidens, nothing can be ruled out completely. And this race had two first-time starters, as well as a horse that had a lot of trouble in his only start. Any of these three runners—as complete unknowns—had the potential to jump up and beat you.

The public was going for Carefree Lover in a big way, betting him down to 4-5. He certainly had some merit. He had run a Beyer of 64 in his first race, but then he had done absolutely nothing when he was moved up to maiden special weight, earning only a 50 speed figure. Now he was being dropped back to maiden claiming $50,000, and he was getting first-time Lasix. The public apparently reasoned that you could throw out his previous race simply because it was against higher-class maidens—even though he had no visible excuse of any kind for his poor performance.

Confess To Me had the clear top Beyer figure by 15 points. He had no obvious negatives. And he was 7-2. He destroyed the field with ease, paying $9.40. A clear case of public neglect. And you had to take advantage of it.

Expensive Passion
Own: Wolf Joan
Royal Blue, White Lightning Bolt, White $8,000
WARNER T (192 13 13 16 .07) 2002:(195 14 .07)

B. m. 5
Sire: Shadow in the Dark (Seattle Slew) $500
Dam: Keene Gal(Nashua)
Br: George Bravo (Pa)
Tr: Desmarais Dennis(62 4 10 5 .06) 2002:(64 4 .06)

L 122

Life	32	M	5	2	$16,355	50	D.Fst 22 0 4 2 $11,385 50
2002	12	M	3	1	$7,680	50	Wet(230) 4 0 0 0 $420 17
2001	13	M	1	1	$3,875	34	Turf(150*) 6 0 1 0 $4,550 42
Pha	26	0	4	2	$11,805	50	Dst(150*) 3 0 0 0 $225 20

14Oct02-4Pha fst 6f	:224 :47 1:001 1:14	3↑ Ⓕ Md 8000 (8-7)	22	2	8	75¼	65½	68½	610	Warner T	L 122 b	2.60	59-30	StrictlyPersonal1194 MagnoliaHall122½ AlwysCrownRoyl1193¼	No factor	9
28Sep02-4Pha fst 5½f	:23 :473 1:003 1:072	3↑ Ⓕ Md 8000 (8-7)	50	8	5	54½	42	31	2no	Warner T	L 122 b	3.50	76-23	Alkeen118no ExpensivePssion1221¾ *StrictlyPersonl*1139	Wide, just missed	8
14Sep02-3Pha fst 6f	:223 :462 :592 1:132	3↑ Ⓕ Md 8000 (8-7)	44	7	3	54	55¼	55	2nk	Warner T	L 122 b	6.10	72-22	Bettrmid118nk ExpnsivPssion122nk WlshSpirit116no	Closed5w, outfinished	7
13Aug02-3Pha fst 6f	:222 :464 1:002 1:14	3↑ Ⓕ Md 8000 (8-7)	17	11	6	52½	1½	21½	710½	Warner T	L 122 b	7.40	59-22	*TrckOrTrth*1182¼ *NmbsTwothosnd*116¾ *VnsDblo*1063¾	3 wide move, empty	11
29Jly02-10Pha fst 5½f	:222 :464 :594 1:064	3↑ Ⓕ Md 8000 (8-7)	29	10	5	53¾	42	33½	26¼	Warner T	L 122 b	25.10	73-20	PuzzlePlce1176¼ ExpensivPssion122nk SntitRosit120¾	Wide, gained place	12
9Jly02-10Pha fst 5½f	:223 :47 1:00 1:064	3↑ Ⓕ Md 8000 (8-7)	25	10	5	65	66	69	66½	Warner T	L 122 fb	46.60	72-17	SweetJennyMc1222¾ *PhoneTheNurse*1221½ MyExWifesAshes120hd	No kick	11
1Jly02-2Pha fst 7f	:224 :464 1:134 1:28	3↑ Ⓕ Md 8000 (8-7)	-0	9	7	72	21½	28	921¾	Warner T	L 122 fb	13.20	41-21	Seattle Key1174¾ Rapture's Report1173½ Ashley's Alibi1134	Wide, tired	12
9Jun02-9Pha fst 6f	:222 :47 1:00 1:133	3↑ Ⓕ Md 8000 (8-7)	19	3	8	85½	66½	58	37¾	Warner T	L 122 fb	34.30	63-21	GoodAndStrmy1205½ *DblThCsh*1102¼ ExpnsvPssn1223	7wd turn, late rally	8
29May02-1Pha fst 7f	:23 :464 1:132 1:27	3↑ Ⓕ Md 8000 (8-7)	20	2	10	94¾	109½	68¼	510½	Warner T	L 123 fb	76.10	57-15	Ruby Lips1234½ Chili Chili1234 *Consilience*123no	Passed tiring rivals	10
13May02-2Pha sly 6f	:222 :471 1:01 1:15	3↑ Ⓕ Md 7000 (8-7)	-0	2	7	4¾	53½	78½	612	Warner T	L 121 fb	45.30	52-30	Please U Me1211 *Carmel Ridge*1163½ Mojetta1213¼	Inside, tired	8

WORKS: Sep11 **Pha 3f fst :381 B** *9/9* Jly26 **Pha 3f fst :373 B** *14/23*
TRAINER: Dirt(133 .07 $1.61) Sprint(72 .04 $0.37) MdnClm(36 .06 $0.80)

If ever they had an election for Most Likely to Bounce, Expensive Passion would be a prime candidate. There was a serious likelihood of her bouncing after her strong effort on September 14. But she ran even better on September 28. Now the chance of her bouncing was even greater. She had all the symptoms:

- She was a 5-year-old mare of very limited ability who had just run a new lifetime-best Beyer.

▶ She had put in a hard, draining effort to earn that new top figure.

▶ She had improved from 17 to 44 to 50, so she fit the "three-and-out" scenario.

▶ She was returning to the races rather quickly, in only 16 days.

▶ Her 50 Beyer was far above her usual figures, which were way down in the 20's.

On October 14 Expensive Passion threw in an extremely dull effort. She raced like an exhausted horse, moving only slightly at one point on the turn and then running out of gas. She finished sixth, losing by 10 lengths. Her Beyer dropped to 22.

Knowwhentofoldthem						
Gr/ro c. 4 (Feb)						

Knowwhentofoldthem is a prime example of speed-figure cycling. When he returned to the races as a 4-year-old on May 5, he ran a huge Beyer—a lifetime-best 88 in a very strenuous effort. He regressed after that, from 74 all the way down to a 35. After a much-needed six-week rest, his Beyers began to recover. When he cleared on the lead on August 19 he was able to run a figure of 77. And then he began a whole new cycle on September 2, and once again he was able to improve up to a 78 Beyer. After that, on October 14, he bounced again down to a 43.

Even with all these predictable dips and rises, Knowwhentofoldthem wasn't able to repeat that 88 Beyer he had run when fresh off a long layoff. It's possible that such an extraordinary effort had set him back permanently. Perhaps some more patient handling would have served him better in the long run. Whatever the case, Knowwhentofoldthem is as dramatic and sustained an illustration of the rhythms of speed-figure cycling as you're ever likely to find. Not many horses repeat this up-and-down pattern over such a lengthy period of time, but the pattern is always worth looking for.

```
8 Super Fuse                          Ch. c. 2 (Apr) ADSSPR02 $38,000                        Life  4 3 0 0 $57,000 99   D.Fst      4 3 0 0 $57,000 99
  Own:Chris Thomas Olrick             Sire: Lite the Fuse (Buckaroo) $7,500                  2002  4 3 0 0 $57,000 99   Wet(345*)  0 0 0 0      $0  –
  Colors Unavailable                  Dam:Season's Flair(D'Accord)                       120 2001  0 M 0 0      $0  –   Turf(215*) 0 0 0 0      $0  –
GONZALEZ C V (–) 2002:(723 77 .11)    Br: Adena Springs (Ky)                                 Aqu   0 0 0 0      $0  –   Dst(400)   2 1 0 0 $27,000 99
                                      Tr: Ciardullo Richard Jr (–) 2002:(270 36 .13)

12Oct02-1Crc fst 6f  :211 :433 :561 1:101 Birdonthewir75k  99 5 2  2hd 13 14½ 14¼ Gonzalez C V 117 b  2.70 93-14 Super Fuse1174¼ Hear No Evil1194½ True Enough1151  Strong hand ride 7
26Sep02-9Crc fst 7f  :23 :463 1:112 1:244 Alw 27000N1X      77 2 6  22 2hd 14 12     Gonzalez C V 118 b  *.60 90-16 Super Fuse1182 Admiral Lance1151½ Don Hector1153¼  Off rail, prevailed 6
31Aug02-6Del fst 6f  :22 :46 :59 1:12     NATC Fty200k      60 12 1 31 2hd 22½ 59¾   Gonzalez C V 116 b *1.30 73-21 CrftyGuy1163 MisterDeux116no CpGoodHop1163½  Stumbled,bid 1/4,faded 12
 3Aug02-9Crc fst 5f  :222 :453 :582       Md Sp Wt 23k      99 10 4 21 2½ 11 14¾     Gonzalez C V 118 b 33.10 97-15 SuperFuse1184¾ MidsEyes1188¾ MillnniumStorm1181¼  Drew away, driving 11
WORKS: Nov8 Crc 5f fst 1:044 B 21/26  Aug22 Crc 4f fst :493 B 6/25
TRAINER: 2YO(87 .14 $2.12) 31-60Days(68 .13 $1.29) Dirt(430 .15 $1.84) Sprint(378 .15 $1.82) Stakes(13 .08 $0.57)
```

If Knowwhentofoldthem best outlines the sustained cycling pattern, then Super Fuse provides the best example of the *perfect* symmetrical cycle. On Festival of the Sun Day at Calder, Super Fuse was among the choices in the $75,000 Birdonthewire. If he could return to the 99 he ran in his first career start he would be unbeatable. He did precisely that, and jogged home in a romp at 5-2.

```
Salt Lake Express                              Ch. c. 4 (May) OBSMAR00 $70,000                       Life  25 5 5 5 $140,890 87   D.Fst     19 4 4 5 $102,990 87
Own: Burnside Charles F                        Sire: Salt Lake (Deputy Minister) $20,000             2002  12 0 3 3  $20,160 78   Wet(380)   5 1 1 0  $36,100 77
Orange Brown Collar/maple Leaf        $10,000  Dam:Fancy Legs(Yukon)                           L 120 2001   8 3 0 2  $69,730 87   Turf(265)  1 0 0 0   $1,800 71
JIMENEZ F M (–) 2002:(296 23 .08)              Br: David J Whelan & Elizabeth P Whelan (Ky)          Pha    0 0 0 0       $0  –   Dst(380)  13 1 3 4  $46,690 85
                                               Tr: Becker Nadine A(11 0 2 2 .00) 2002:(170 19 .11)

28Oct02-3Del fst 1   :25 :492 1:143 1:403 3+ Clm 8000(8-7)        76 4 22½ 23 22 23 2no     Fogelsonger R5 L 113     3.80 79-22 DakotaAppeal118no SaltLkeExpress1137¾ Brgin1182¼ Finished well, missed 6
13Oct02-4Del wf 6f   :222 :46 :584 1:113 3+ Clm 6250(6.25-6)     64 3 7 72 62¼ 54 45¼      Clifton T      L 118    34.40 80-14 Rockdale115½ Counter Bid1204 Seattle's Fortune118¾  Rallied mildly 8
30Sep02-9Del fst 6f  :223 :462 :592 1:122 3+ Clm c-5000           58 1 4 21 43 42½ 54       Jones S R      L 118    10.00 77-17 Wallace118¾ Lazorato1202¾ Heroic Peace118½  Chased, gave way 11
  Claimed from Blue Willow Stable for $5,000, Hanford Gail M Trainer 2002(as of 09/30): ( 12 0 0 0 0.00 )
10Sep02-6Del fst 6f  :221 :453 :582 1:11 3+ Clm 10000(10-9)       56 1 6 63½ 65½ 66¾ 514   Unsihuay A     L 118     4.60 74-19 Wise Talk1183¼ Cara Rubiano1206¾ Malinverno116½  No threat 8
 3Sep02-4Del fst 170 :24 :482 1:133 1:431 3+ Clm 12500(12.5-10.5) 53 5 1½ 11 2hd 43 717      Unsihuay A     L 118 f   5.80 68-22 Vilar1183¾ Mount Vesuvio1206½ Dustin's Dozer1181  Vied for 3/4, tired 9
21Jly02-1Del fst 6f  :22 :453 :584 1:114 3+ Clm c-(10-9)          75 11 115 84½ 62½ 31¼    Dominguez R A  L 118 fb  4.10 83-13 NouveuRich116nk LvItToBzr1181 SltLkExprss1181¼  Rail, came out, closed 11
  Claimed from Schnably Michael for $10,000, Runco Jeff C Trainer 2002(as of 07/21): ( 402 64 49 52 0.16 )
30Jun02-6Del fst 6f  :22 :451 :582 1:12 3+ Clm c-(10-9)           75 1 6 32 34 22½ 22¾      Martin E M Jr  L 118 b   3.40 80-20 Gadir1182¾ SaltLakeExpress1181¾ TrpperMeek1182¼  Rail bid, needed more 9
  Claimed from Russell Riggins for $10,000, Pino Michael V Trainer 2002(as of 06/30): ( 147 35 22 18 0.24 )
 5Jun02-4Del fst 6f  :22 :451 :573 1:103 3+ Clm c-(12.5-10.5)     68 5 3 32½ 33 26 39¼      McCarthy M J   L 118 f  *1.50 81-12 Fleety1189 Seemslikeyesterday119nk SltLkeExpress1183¾  Bid, outfinished 7
  Claimed from Cohen Philip & Marcia & Klesaris St for $12,500, Klesaris Steve Trainer 2002(as of 06/05): ( 94 13 17 22 0.14 )
11May02-1Del fst 6f  :22 :453 :583 1:114 3+ Clm 10000(10-9)       78 1 3 23½ 22½ 21½ 2¾     Bartram B E    L 116 f   2.80 83-17 Appellnt116¾ SltLkeExpress1162¼ LeveItToBezr1162½  Angled out, gaining 6
27Apr02-5Del fst 6f  :22 :453 :583 1:114 3+ Clm 16000(16-14)      64 1 6 74¾ 73¾ 64¼ 75     Bartram B E    L 116     4.80 79-13 Dry Ice119nk Brass Bo1161¼ Big Time Flyer116¾  Lacked a rally 11
TRAINER: Route/Sprint(35 .06 $0.47) Dirt(345 .09 $1.02) Sprint(256 .08 $0.93) Claim(258 .09 $1.01)
```

On October 28, 2002, Salt Lake Express was entered in a mile race at Delaware Park. A quick glance at his past performances would lead you to one seemingly inescapable conclusion: This horse can't go a distance. On September 3 he had tried one mile and 70 yards and had collapsed in the stretch. His Beyer in that distance race was his lowest in his last 10 starts. In addition, his sire, Salt Lake, is best known for speed horses and sprinters.

An open-and-shut case. Or so it appeared at first glance. But a deeper look at his running style and, more especially, his Beyer-figure pattern, would warn you not to jump to any conclusions about the distance ability of Salt Lake Express. First, the two-turn race on September 3 had come after a six-week layoff and Salt Lake Express had run head and head for the lead. Since his best running seemed to be done from off the pace, he at least had some excuse for that poor effort. Second, he had run back-to-back Beyers of 75 before that distance race—quite big Beyers at that stage in his career. A regression from those two efforts, combined with the six-week layoff and a radical change in running style, all combined to make me suspend judgment about how effectively Salt Lake Express could handle two turns. Perhaps you couldn't bet him in this race, but I also couldn't eliminate him.

Salt Lake Express handled the two turns brilliantly. He ran a Beyer of 76, and only fell short by a nose in trying to catch a loafing speed horse. His case proves just how costly and misleading snap judgments can be. A more careful, in-depth look at past performances, and a sophisticated analysis of Beyer Speed Figure patterns, can help you avoid the kind of thinking that would have thrown out Salt Lake Express without a second thought.

3 Shotgun Fire
Own:Cherry Martin L
Red, Red Cherries On White Ball, Red
GARCIA J A (79 12 10 9 .15) 2002:(483 84 .17)

Ch. c. 4 (Feb) BARMAR00 $150,000
Sire: Out of Place (Cox's Ridge) $17,500
Dam:Shot Gun Frances(Commemorate)
Br: Edna Follin (Fla)
Tr: Wolfson Martin D(14 4 3 2 .29) 2002:(166 33 .20)

L 122

Life	12	2	2	0	$51,160	83	D.Fst	8	1	1	0	$28,060	82
2002	10	2	2	0	$51,160	83	Wet(320)	3	1	1	0	$23,100	83
2001	2	M	0	0	$0	57	Turf(275)	1	0	0	0	$0	48
Crc Ⓣ	0	0	0	0	$0	–	DstⓉ(315)	0	0	0	0	$0	–

1Nov02-4Crc	gd	$1\frac{1}{16}$		:23^4	:48^3	1:13^3	1:47^3	3↑	OClm 16000(16-14)N	83	1	2^1	1^{hd}	$1^{1\frac{1}{2}}$	$1^{2\frac{1}{2}}$	$1^{1\frac{1}{2}}$	Cruz M R	L 119	*1.70	74-28	ShotgunFire$119^{1\frac{1}{2}}$ **It'sANewMoon**$119^{3\frac{1}{4}}$ MjorMecke118^1	Off rail, prevailed	8
12Oct02-4Crc	fst	6f		:21^2	:44^2	:57^2	1:10^2	3↑	Alw 27000N1X	68	1	6	4^2	4^3	5^4	$5^{10\frac{1}{2}}$	Cruz M R	L 119	5.20	81-14	*Virtual Zone*115^2 Friendly Frolic$115^{\frac{3}{4}}$ Stuff Shot$110^{7\frac{1}{2}}$	Faltered	8
Previously trained by Kimmel John C																							
7Sep02-5Med	fst	6f		:21^4	:44^2	:56^2	1:09	3↑	Alw 30000N1X	39	3	2	1^{hd}	$4^{1\frac{1}{4}}$	7^{10}	$7^{17\frac{1}{2}}$	Coa E M	L 118 f	2.60	77-06	Power Wing118^{nk} Chariot$118^{\frac{1}{2}}$ Worth Springs118^{hd}	Dueled inside,faltered	8
15Aug02-8Mth	fst	6f		:21^3	:44	:56^2	1:09^3	3↑	Alw 33000N1X	82	4	2	$2^{\frac{1}{2}}$	2^1	$2^{2\frac{1}{2}}$	$2^{4\frac{1}{2}}$	Coa E M	L 120 f	*1.20	86-14	HighCascde$120^{4\frac{1}{2}}$ ShotgunFire120^3 StormyDy115^{13}	Fast pace,chased lane	5
7Jun02-7Bel	wf	$1\frac{1}{16}$		:23	:45^1	1:08^3	1:40	3↑	Alw 46000N1X	78	6	$2^{\frac{1}{2}}$	$2^{1\frac{1}{2}}$	3^2	4^{10}	5^{12}	Castellano J J	L 121	66.00	88-02	Wild Years121^3 Bakhoor$118^{4\frac{1}{2}}$ *Gyrfalcon*$121^{2\frac{3}{4}}$	Chased outside, tired	7
22May02-8Bel	fst	6f		:23	:46^2	:58^1	1:10^2	3↑	Alw 45000N1X	78	8	3	$3^{\frac{1}{2}}$	2^{hd}	$3^{\frac{1}{2}}$	5^3	Castellano J J	L 122	45.25	83-15	Aggadan$116^{\frac{3}{4}}$ Stone Age$122^{1\frac{3}{4}}$ Amjaad122^{no}	Bumped upper stretch	8
12Apr02-8Aqu	fm	$1\frac{1}{16}$	Ⓣ	:22^3	:47^3	1:11^4	1:43^4	3↑	Alw 44000N1X	48	4	$2^{3\frac{1}{2}}$	2^{hd}	2^1	9^{18}	$10^{19\frac{3}{4}}$	Migliore R	L 122	16.10	65-15	Robbie'sRockin111^2 Glmdring$114^{3\frac{1}{4}}$ PreferrdGust$119^{\frac{3}{4}}$	Chased pace, tired	10
16Mar02-10GP	fst	$1\frac{1}{16}$		:22^4	:46^3	1:11	1:43^2	4↑	Alw 34000N1X	67	7	$4^{3\frac{1}{2}}$	5^4	$7^{4\frac{3}{4}}$	8^8	$9^{16\frac{3}{4}}$	Santos J A	L 118	17.40	74-08	Jckpot$118^{\frac{1}{2}}$ *UnbridledVision*$122^{4\frac{1}{2}}$ *DteMoreMinors*118^6	Early foot, faded	11
16Feb02-12GP	wf	$1\frac{1}{8}$	⊗	:47^1	1:13	1:41^1	1:54^2	4↑	Alw 34000N1X	64	3	$1^{\frac{1}{2}}$	$1^{\frac{1}{2}}$	1^1	1^2	2^3	Bailey J D	L 118 f	*1.00	62-23	SmthsonVlly120^3 ShotgunFr$118^{1\frac{1}{2}}$ SprklOtFront$118^{\frac{3}{4}}$	Inside, outfinished	11
21Jan02-5GP	fst	7f		:22^4	:46	1:12	1:25^2	4	Md Sp Wt 32k	77	9	6	$5^{1\frac{1}{4}}$	3^1	$2^{1\frac{1}{2}}$	$1^{3\frac{1}{4}}$	Velazquez J R	L 122	7.60	80-23	Shotgun Fire$122^{3\frac{1}{4}}$ Cabot Trail$122^{\frac{1}{2}}$ *Ochoco*$122^{1\frac{1}{2}}$	Drew clear late	10

WORKS: Nov20 **Crc 4f fst :50 B** *15/31* ●Oct27 **Crc 4f fst :49 B** *1/27* Oct21 **Crc 5f fst 1:02 B** *2/20* Oct6 **Crc 5f fst 1:05^2 B** *20/20* Sep5 **Mth 3f fst :38 B** *5/9* Aug27 **Mth 4f fst :49 B** *5/21*
TRAINER: Dirt/Turf(41 .20 $1.73) Turf(140 .18 $1.87) Routes(228 .22 $1.80) Alw(110 .24 $1.77)

Shotgun Fire also doesn't look like much of a distance horse. He consistently tires after seven furlongs or a mile, and he has only one second-place finish in four races beyond seven furlongs. But, just as with Salt Lake Express, a more careful look at his Beyer figures gives a very different view.

The figure of 64 that he ran back in February at Gulfstream does not look encouraging. But he could have regressed somewhat after running a big Beyer of 77 following a layoff. The clinching evidence, however, comes in the races of May 22 and June 7. At six furlongs in May he earned a Beyer of 78. At $1\frac{1}{16}$ miles in June he earned the same 78. The fact that he lost that distance race by 12 lengths gives the appearance that he couldn't handle the distance. But the Beyer figure says otherwise. He ran equally fast sprinting and routing.

On November 1, Shotgun Fire had no trouble with the $1\frac{1}{16}$-mile distance. He won by $1\frac{1}{2}$ lengths with a Beyer of 83.

2 Brocco Bob
Own:Brockley Thomas
Green, Orange Circle, Purple 'b', Purple
CASTELLANO J J (73 4 9 18 .05) 2002:(854 122 .14)

Dk. b or br g. 4 (Feb) KEENOV98 $20,000
Sire: Brocco (Kris S.) $875
Dam:Inaruckus(Bold Ruckus)
Br: Patricia Staskowski Purdy (NY)
Tr: Galluscio Dominic G(5 0 0 1 .00) 2002:(178 26 .15)

L 121

Life	18	4	2	2	$119,670	87	D.Fst	12	1	2	2	$51,330	87
2002	8	2	1	0	$46,050	87	Wet(290)	4	3	0	0	$65,700	82
2001	7	1	1	2	$47,790	82	Turf(200)	2	0	0	0	$2,640	75
Bel	3	0	0	0	$5,280	76	Dst(285)	9	3	1	1	$73,880	87

2Sep02-2Sar	fst	6f		:22^4	:46^1	:58^3	1:11^4	3↑	Clm 25000	87	2	3	$1^{\frac{1}{2}}$	$1^{\frac{1}{2}}$	$1^{2\frac{1}{2}}$	1no	Castellano J J	L 118 fb	5.20	83-16	Brocco Bob118^{no} *Cliff Notes*$114^{\frac{1}{2}}$ Rich Coins121^3	Pace, clear, held on	8
17Aug02-2Sar	my	6f		:22^2	:45^4	:58^1	1:11^2	3↑	Clm c-20000	81	4	4	$1^{4\frac{1}{2}}$	$1^{3\frac{1}{2}}$	1^5	$1^{1\frac{1}{2}}$	Smith M E	L 116 fb	*1.70	85-11	*Brocco Bob*$116^{1\frac{1}{2}}$ Above The Crowd$114^{1\frac{3}{4}}$ RichCoins$121^{2\frac{1}{4}}$	Set pace, driving	6
Claimed from Seven Pin Stables for $20,000, Terranova John P II Trainer 2002(as of 08/17): (100 13 18 12 0.13)																							
25Jly02-6Sar	fst	6f		:22^2	:45^2	:58	1:10^4	3↑	Ⓢ Alw 45000N2X	82	5	2	1^{hd}	1^{hd}	3^{nk}	$4^{2\frac{1}{4}}$	Gryder A T	L 122 b	11.90	86-13	Papua$117^{\frac{3}{4}}$ **Salute Him**$122^{\frac{1}{2}}$ **Mister Bravo**117^1	Set pace, tired	7
26Jun02-7Bel	fst	6f		:22^2	:45^1	:57^1	1:09^4	3↑	Ⓢ Alw 45000N2X	66	1	4	4^7	$4^{5\frac{1}{2}}$	$4^{8\frac{1}{2}}$	$5^{9\frac{1}{4}}$	Velazquez J R	L 122 b	4.30	80-10	Le Bourget$122^{6\frac{1}{2}}$ Decisive122^{nk} **Mister Bravo**$116^{1\frac{1}{4}}$	Wide, no response	7
12Jun02-7Bel	fst	7f		:22^3	:45^4	1:10	1:22^4	3↑	Ⓢ Alw 45000N2X	76	6	2	$2^{\frac{1}{2}}$	$2^{\frac{1}{2}}$	3^8	$4^{7\frac{1}{4}}$	Gryder A T	L 121 b	15.20	82-17	*Value Line*121^4 Smokieisabandit115^3 **Y Two J**110^{nk}	Speed 3 wide, tired	7
23Feb02-6Aqu	fst	6f	⊡	:23	:45^4	:57^4	1:10^2	4↑	Ⓢ Alw 45000N2X	72	5	8	4^1	$4^{5\frac{1}{2}}$	4^{11}	6^9	Gryder A T	L 120 fb	5.80	83-13	ConmnCnnnghm$120^{3\frac{1}{4}}$ BtThGtTony118^3 RnnngTody118^1	Posed no threat	10
3Feb02-5Aqu	fst	6f	⊡	:23^1	:46^3	:58^4	1:11^2	4↑	Ⓢ Alw 45000N2X	83	3	3	$2^{\frac{1}{2}}$	$2^{\frac{1}{2}}$	2^2	$2^{1\frac{1}{4}}$	Gryder A T	L 120 fb	4.20	86-16	StrikThBrss$123^{1\frac{1}{4}}$ BroccoBob120^1 DistntDibo118^1	With pace, good finish	7
9Jan02-7Aqu	sly	6f	⊡	:22^2	:45^4	:58^2	1:11^3	4↑	Ⓢ Alw 45000N2X	71	2	5	$4^{1\frac{1}{2}}$	$3^{2\frac{1}{2}}$	$3^{2\frac{1}{2}}$	4^4	Velez J A Jr	L 123 fb	4.60	82-14	Coast ToCoast$118^{2\frac{3}{4}}$ GoBigBlue$118^{\frac{1}{2}}$ JustJustin$118^{\frac{3}{4}}$	Inside trip, no punch	8
14Dec01-9Aqu	gd	6f	⊡	:23^1	:47	:59^3	1:13	3↑	Ⓢ Alw 43000N1X	82	1	8	2^{hd}	$1^{\frac{1}{2}}$	$1^{1\frac{1}{2}}$	$1^{\frac{3}{4}}$	Gryder A T	L 117 fb	3.40	80-21	Brocco Bob$117^{\frac{3}{4}}$ Flo's Charm118^1 ***Salute Him***$117^{\frac{1}{2}}$	Clear,then steady drv	11
26Aug01-7Sar	fst	7f		:22^4	:46	1:11	1:24	3↑	Ⓢ Alw 43000N1X	74	5	3	3^{nk}	2^{hd}	2^{hd}	$2^{3\frac{1}{2}}$	Bailey J D	L 116 b	*2.05	81-12	Go Big Blue$116^{3\frac{1}{2}}$ *Brocco Bob*$116^{\frac{1}{2}}$ River Spirit116^2	Vied 3 wide, gamely	8
8Aug01-9Sar	fst	7f		:22^2	:45^3	1:11^4	1:25	3↑	Ⓢ Alw 43000N1X	74	6	10	4^2	$4^{1\frac{1}{2}}$	1^{hd}	$3^{3\frac{3}{4}}$	Bailey J D	L 116 b	*2.00	76-15	*Tortellini Ted*120^1 ValueLine$116^{2\frac{3}{4}}$ BroccoBob$116^{\frac{1}{2}}$	Awkward start, 3 wide	10
23Jun01-5Bel	fm	$1\frac{1}{8}$	[T]	:48^2	1:13	1:38	1:50^2	3↑	Ⓢ Alw 44000N1X	70	3	$1^{\frac{1}{2}}$	$1^{\frac{1}{2}}$	1^{hd}	3^{nk}	$8^{4\frac{3}{4}}$	Migliore R	L 116 b	2.45	72-20	Haggs Castle116^{nk} Morganite121^{hd} Hendler$121^{1\frac{1}{2}}$	Speed inside, tired	10

WORKS: Sep22 **Bel 4f fst :51^2 B** *40/44* Jly17 **Sar tr.tⓉ 4f hd :48 B** *2/12*
TRAINER: Dirt(364 .17 $1.72) Sprint(217 .16 $1.90) Alw(100 .14 $1.29)

The examples of Salt Lake Express and Shotgun Fire demonstrate the value of careful Beyer profiling in helping to determine how far a horse might want to run. The same is true in determining wet-track ability.

There are many, many cases just like Brocco Bob's. A superficial look tells you that he could be a "wet-track horse." But is he really? While he is 3 for 4 in wet-track races, his Beyer figures show no difference at all between his dry-track figures and wet-track figures. He's as good on one as he is on the other. Next time you come across a horse with a wet-track record like Brocco Bob's, take a careful look at his Beyer figures. You'll find that the true wet-track horse—the one who actually runs consistently faster on wet surfaces—is a very rare species indeed.

Burning Roma
Own: Queen Harold L

B. h. 4 FTFFEB00 $40,000
Sire: Rubiano (Fappiano) $10,000
Dam: While Rome Burns(Overskate)
Br: William S Farish Jr (Ky)
Tr: Giglio Heather A (—) 2002:(99 17 .17)

Life	23	10	2	5	$1,205,537	114	
2002	9	2	1	2	$350,237	107	
2001	9	5	1	3	$614,000	114	
CSC	0	0	0	0	$0	–	
D.Fst	22	9	2	5	$1,085,537	108	
Wet(330)	1	1	0	0	$120,000	114	
Turf(295)	0	0	0	0	$0	–	
Dist	0	0	0	0	$0	–	

5Nov02-8Aqu fst 1⅛ :47 1:113 1:371 1:502 3↑ Stuyvesant-G3 **83** 8 1hd 1hd 3nk 73¼ 1011¾ Coa E M L 120 3.25 72-16 *Snake Mountain*114½ Windsor Castle1151¼ *Docent*1153¼ Vied inside, tired 10
4Oct02-8Med fst 1⅛ :464 1:102 1:353 1:484 3↑ Med Cup H-G2 **107** 2 31 1½ 1½ 11½ 1¾ Coa E M L 115 13.20 83-19 Burning Roma115¾ *Volponi*1161¼ Windsor Castle112nk Clear,drifted out 9
13Sep02-8Med fst 1 1/16 :233 :472 1:111 1:431 3↑ Alysheba50k **105** 3 31½ 2hd 12 13 16¼ Coa E M L 113 *.90 90-16 *BurnngRom*1136¼ Pckpspd113nk BknownToM1156½ Clear,moderate urging 5
20Aug02-7Del fst 1 1/16 :233 :47 1:111 1:444 3↑ Red Dog57k **63** 2 34 45½ 46½ 511 522¼ Martin E M Jr L 116 *1.20 62-23 Confucius Say1164¾ Marciano1201¾ *Jarf*1204¾ Dull effort 5
10Aug02-7Mnr fst 1 1/16 :232 :461 1:102 1:421 3↑ WVaGovnorsH88k **102** 7 45½ 33 11 1hd 2nk Martin E M Jr LB 122 *1.70 97-07 Docent114nk Burning Roma122½ X Country12112 In tandem, out gamed 7
29Jun02-7Del fst 1 :241 :474 1:121 1:371 3↑ Brandywine100k **89** 1 65 45 46½ 49½ 612½ McCarthy M J L 116 *.80 83-20 H'sAKnockout1163 Mrcino1167¾ Bu'sSurpris116hd Steaded early,no factr 7
Previously trained by Mott William I
27May02-9Bel fst 1 :222 :443 1:083 1:331 3↑ MetropoltnH-G1 **94** 10 71¾ 73¾ 65½ 613 714½ Prado E S L 116 8.50 88 — SweptOverboard1174¾ Aldebaran1151½ CraftyC.T.1164¼ 5 wide, no response 10
13Apr02-9Aqu fst 7f :214 :432 1:08 1:214 3↑ Carter H-G1 **107** 7 8 99¾ 911 63¾ 31¾ Bailey J D L 117 3.75 89-12 Affirmed Success1191 Voodoo113¾ Burning Roma1171¼ In tight stretch 10
9Mar02-10GP fst 7f :22 :443 1:091 1:221 3↑ GP BC H-G2 **101** 6 7 67 65½ 63¼ 31¾ Prado E S L 118 4.60 94-12 Dream Run1131½ Binthebest114nk BurningRoma118hd Mild rally, up for 3rd 8
Previously trained by Dutrow Anthony W
19Oct01-8Med fst 1⅛ :451 1:084 1:34 1:462 Pegasus H-G2 **108** 5 32 31 3½ 3nk 22¾ Bailey J D L 119 *1.30 92-14 Volponi1142¾ BurningRom119½ GintGentlemn1169½ Dueled,weakened 1/16 6
WORKS: Oct29 Del 4f fst :482 B *2/39* **●Sep29 Del 5f fst 1:003 B** *1/14*

Some horses don't fit neatly into any of the patterns described earlier in these pages, but they do conform to a clear pattern of their own—a particular individual Beyer pattern. For example, except on one occasion, every time Burning Roma ran a Beyer in the triple digits, he regressed immediately afterward. On November 5 at Aqueduct in the Stuyvesant Handicap he was coming off just such a huge Beyer of 107, earned in a very stressful effort. He bounced as badly as a horse can bounce, dueling for the lead, and then stopping nearly to a walk in the stretch. He finished last.

5	**Wish From Heaven**		Ch. c. 2 (Mar) OBSAPR02 $16,000					Life	6 M 1 1		$3,890 50	D.Fst	6 0 1 1		$3,890 50
	Own:Morises Farm		Sire: Heaven's Wish (Halo) $1,000					2002	6 M 1 1		$3,890 50	Wet(309)	0 0 0 0		$0 –
	Hot Pink, White Circled M, Hot Pink Cap	$16,000	Dam:Luckywaki(Lucky North)					2001	0 M 0 0		$0 –	Turf(267)	0 0 0 0		$0 –
	HOMEISTER R B JR (460 62 61 65 .13) 2002:(552 71 .13)		Br: John Franks (Fla)				L 118									
			Tr: Estevez Manuel A(90 15 14 12 .17) 2002:(139 19 .14)					Crc	6 0 1 1		$3,890 50	Dst(299)	4 0 0 1		$1,790 50

26Sep02-10Crc	fst	5f	:22² :47¹	1:00³	Md 16000 (16 –14)		20 5 7	7⁴	64½ 67½ 89½	Cruz M R	L 118 b	2.90	76 – 16	CntrlCmmnd118¹HsNtBlffn118³½HndsmHnr118¾	Bumped start, faltered 10
8Sep02- 1Crc	fst	5f	:22⁴ :47¹	1:00²	Md 16000 (16 –14)		50 1 4	1hd	11 11½ 3nk	Homeister R B Jr	L 118 b	2.80	87 – 15	YourMgicl118no SpeclTour118nk WishFromHeven118²¾	Off rail, just failed 6
16Aug02- 3Crc	fst	5½f	:22² :46⁴	.59³ 1:06¹	Md 16000 (16 –14)		22 3 8	43½	4⁴ 57¼ 51³	Cruz M R	118 b	3.70	78 – 11	JudgHrpr118½FloridCowboy118⁸ H'snoctor118¹⅓	Bumped start, faltered 9
23Jly02-10Crc	fst	6f	:22³ :47	1:00⁴ 1:15¹	Md 16000 (16 –14)		16 10 3	52¼	55 5⁴ 66½	Cruz M R	118	11.40	62 – 14	Quiet Tipper118no Rageously118³ Umcane116½	3 wide, lacked a rally 10
4Jly02- 3Crc	fst	5½f	:22² :46³	1:00³ 1:07⁴	Md 25000 (25 –22.5)		20 2 7	53½	76½ 87⅞ 89	Cruz M R	118	11.60	74 – 11	IndianCrusader118hd TouchdownRun118¹ ParisCper118²	On rail, faltered 12
18Jun02- 3Crc	fst	4½f	:23² :47²	:53³	Md 16000 (16 –14)		19 4 5	42½	2⁶ 2¹⁰½	Cruz M R	118	4.70	80 – 09	CrusdingKip113¹⁰WishFromHeven118nk FrdNAnni118hd	Off slowly, 3 wide 6

WORKS: Sep1 Crc 4f fst :49² B 5/31 Aug11 Crc 5f fst 1:04² B 14/15 Aug3 Crc 3f fst :37³ Bg 15/42 Jly16 Crc 4f fst :50² B 21/35
TRAINER: 2YO(129 .09 $1.33) Dirt(353 .12 $1.54) Sprint(241 .12 $1.69) MdnClm(148 .08 $1.31)

At Calder Race Course, low-level maiden-claiming races are as common as weeds, especially for the seemingly endless population of statebred 2-year-olds. In this particular race on September 26, a 2-year-old colt named Wish From Heaven was one of the obvious choices, and, were it not for a hot first-time starter, he would have been the clear favorite in this 10-horse event.

Wish From Heaven was far and away the top Beyer figure in the field. His last-race figure of 50 was more than 22 points higher than anyone else's. But he was suspect. After floundering around in his first four races, encountering minor trouble but never running more than a Beyer of 22, he had suddenly taken heavy money in his last start, along with an apparently quite beneficial dose of Lasix. Unfortunately, he ended up in a duel for the lead with three other horses. Still, he held on gamely, and jumped way up to a Beyer of 50—far beyond any of his previous mediocre efforts. And there was a little twist to that race that made Wish From Heaven even more attractive to some players, especially "key-race" enthusiasts: Two of the horses he had battled with on the front end had already come back to win in their next starts. So why shouldn't Wish From Heaven do the same?

The answer was clear: The Beyer-figure patterns for the other two horses were as different from Wish From Heaven's as they could be. Ringaliyo, for example, had debuted with a figure of 24 in a $25,000 maiden claimer. He had then been dropped down to a $16,000 race, where he dueled with Wish From Heaven and tired in the late stages. His Beyer improved to a 41. Then he dropped even farther down to a $12,500 maiden claimer, where he prevailed on a sloppy track, earning a winning Beyer of 52. Ringaliyo's figures had improved gradually—24-41-52—as he worked his way down to a level where he could win. The other winner, Looney Lionel, had made his first start in the September 8 race, joining in the duel with Wish From Heaven and Ringaliyo. He faded to a Beyer of 39 in that race. Then he was dropped to a $12,500 maiden claimer and won with a figure of 44. Clearly there was nothing very surprising or dramatic in either Ringaliyo's or Looney Lionel's brief career.

But Wish From Heaven's story was very different, and very negative. As an obviously unaccomplished 2-year-old, he received first-time Lasix, was bet heavily, and ran an all-out, exhausting effort dueling for the lead the entire way to the wire, losing by only a neck. That represented a huge improvement over all his previous races. Unlike Ringaliyo and Looney Lionel, he was a seriously bad risk in his next start. Occasionally a horse like this will fool you and follow up with another strong race, but not very often. And even if he does, the price will almost always be too short in proportion to the risk.

On September 26 Wish From Heaven raced sluggishly, never made a move, and finished a distant eighth, 9½ lengths behind. His Beyer dropped to a 20. He was the close second choice at 5-2. The hot firster won it all.

7 Father Mark			

The case of Father Mark leads us along a number of lines of inquiry. As in his previous race on September 15, he once again looked like the clear lone speed on September 25, and at the identical distance of one mile. His competition was weak, and he had the clear top Beyer figure. So what's not to like?

1. The Beyer pattern of Father Mark had to give you pause. Not many horses have this kind of persistent good-fig/bad-fig pattern for seven races over a span of as long as three months. Every time he ran a figure in the 70's, he followed that with a much poorer figure. And on September 25 he was coming off a figure of 72. Would he put in another weaker effort?

2. The great mitigating circumstance for Father Mark was the fact that he would very likely be in front by himself, as he was in his previous win. When a horse gets an easy trip, without much unusual stress—when he doesn't have to extend himself fully—he has a much better chance of repeating a good effort.

3. But does Father Mark really want to run a mile? His two seven-furlong races resulted in much weaker figures. His best figures are at six furlongs. And his recent mile figure of 72 was earned under the most optimal conditions possible. But, even if one mile is not his best distance, he might still be able to persevere once again by controlling the race on the front end.

4. Although his trainer had been doing well at Delaware, he was taking this horse from major outfits in the mid-Atlantic. Father Mark was not likely to improve in his new surroundings.

Doubts about Father Mark's chances on September 25 arose principally from his questionable Beyer-figure pattern. And these doubts were supplemented by some skepticism about his distance ability and his recent trainer change. I could certainly understand why some would pronounce Father Mark unbeatable as the top figure and the lone speed, but, at odds of 4-5, there were enough reasons for questioning his chances. You might not want to bet against him, but he was very suspect at the price.

On September 25 Father Mark loafed along on a fairly easy, slow-to-moderate pace, and then weakened late in the stretch. He was passed by two other horses. Just as in his previous efforts, after he ran a figure in the 70's he regressed. His Beyer fell back to a 60.

1a Warlock's Crypt
Own:Sammy G Stable
Black, Silver 'sg', Silver Sleeves
OTTS C L (686 120 95 78 .17) 2002:(707 123 .17)

$16,000

B. c. 3 (Apr) KEESEP00 $25,000
Sire: Storm Boot (Storm Cat) $15,000
Dam: Risen Witch(Conquistador Cielo)
Br: Upson Downs Farm & James Ernst (Ky)
Tr: Lake Scott A(287 76 47 32 .26) 2002:(1473 325 .22)

L 117

Life	20	4	3	1	$74,715	87	D.Fst	18	4	3	1	$74,715	87
2002	13	4	3	1	$74,285	87	Wet(320)	2	0	0	0	$0	44
2001	7	M	0	0	$430	44	Turf(295)	0	0	0	0	$0	–
Del	5	1	2	0	$35,070	87	Dst(340)	12	3	3	0	$60,900	87

9Oct02-3Del	fst	6f	:223	:461	:584	1:103	Clm c-(16-14)	68	6	1	22	31	33½	410¾	Caraballo J C	L 117 b	*2.10	79-15	Huber Woods1198¼ **FatherMark**1172¼ MinersRelief119nk	Chased, weakened	7
Claimed from Campanella Vince for $16,000, Cox Kenneth M Trainer 2002(as of 10/09): (108 11 21 19 0.10)																					
8Sep02-5Del	fst	6f	:231	:471	1:00	1:124	Clm c-(16-14)	74	7	1	1hd	2hd	1½	2½	Castillo O O	L 119 b	*1.50	78-22	LttlMrshll119½ Wrlck'sCrypt1194¼ BlshngJdth1171¾	Short lead,just failed	7
Claimed from Toscano John T Jr for $16,000, Lake Scott A Trainer 2002(as of 09/08): (1168 261 205 148 0.22)																					
2Aug02-1Sar	fst	7f	:233	:471	1:12	1:244	Clm 25000	60	4	6	71½	65½	49½	510¼	Carrero V5	L 116 b	3.10	71-20	MightyGulch1192¼ AllGeredUp119¾ *MisterSilence*1216¼	Wide trip, no rally	9
3Jly02-6Pha	fst	6f	:213	:443	:571	1:102	Clm 25000(25-20)	81	1	8	71½	51½	1½	12¼	Flores J L	L 120 b	*.80	87-12	Wrlock'sCrypt1202¼ GothmLimited1204¼ AdmirlAlbert120½	Outside, clear	9
9Jly02-6Del	fst	6f	:22	:453	:584	1:121	Clm 25000(25-20)	75	5	7	72½	62½	33½	21¾♦	Dominguez R A	L 119 b	*1.40	80-18	*Orka*1171¾ [DH] *Leo's Kayo*117 [DH] *Warlock'sCrypt*119¾	Closed to share 2nd	8
Previously trained by Brooks Gerald E																					
9Jun02-1Bel	fst	7f	:224	:453	1:10	1:231	Clm 35000(35-25)	66	2	5	62¼	76¾	38½	35	Toscano P R	L 121 b	*1.90	82-10	Whisk1211 Dr. Can Do1174 Warlock's Crypt1214	Bumped backstretch	7
Previously trained by Lake Scott A																					
2Jun02-6Del	fst	6f	:214	:451	:582	1:112	Clm 35000(35-30)	87	6	6	62½	42¼	2½	12½	Dominguez R A	L 118 b	3.20	86-18	Warlock's Crypt1182½ Radio One1183¼ Leo's Kayo118¾	Closed, drove clear	7
2May02-8Del	fst	6f	:213	:444	:58	1:11	Alw 41600N2X	68	2	5	63½	75½	65	57¾	Potts C L	L 119 b	6.00	80-13	*RunningTide*1164¼ LordAbounding1161 GoldPhantom1162	Lacked a rally	7
8Apr02-8Pha	fst	6f	:214	:443	:573	1:113	Alw 22480N1X	73	3	2	52½	42½	31½	1hd	Madrigal R Jr	L 119 b	*2.10	81-16	Wrlock'sCrypt119hd *HouseMony*1221¾ *RB'sBoy*119no	Angled out4w,in time	7
5Mar02-9Pha	fst	6½f	:213	:444	1:11	1:18	Clm 25000(25-20)	72	3	4	32	3nk	13	16¾	Flores J L	L 120 b	2.10	85-19	*Warlock's Crypt*1206¾ *Babinsky*1202¼ PipeBomb1201	Bid turn,steady drive	6

RAINER: 1stClaim(344 .23 $1.86) Dirt(2810 .25 $1.73) Sprint(1998 .26 $1.88) Claim(1749 .26 $1.75)

Warlock's Crypt raises important issues concerning the relationship between trainer changes, stressful races, and speed-figure patterns. After his September 8 race his Beyer pattern strongly suggested a movement in the direction of his 81 figure earned on July 23. But there were two cautionary flags:

1. Warlock's Crypt was claimed by a very minor trainer from a very major player. The previous trainer, Scott Lake, had dropped the horse down to $16,000 in order to win another race and the horse had not run again for five weeks, with no published workouts.
2. In his previous race, Warlock's Crypt had been involved in an uncharacteristic duel for the lead through the entire six furlongs. There are many cases like this, where a horse appears to be in the midst of a figure cycle, but the extreme stress of the last race makes you wonder what effect it will have on the

horse's ability to improve again in his next start. No such problem intervened in Warlock's Crypt's earlier cycle, from an 87 down to a 66, up to a 75 (earned under not very stressful conditions) and then to an 81 on July 23. There can be no hard-and-fast rule here. It's a judgment call. But, in this particular case, with the "negative" trainer change added to the unusually draining race on September 8 and the substantial layoff, the better part of wisdom would recommend a pass on Warlock's Crypt.

On October 9 Warlock's Crypt was run off his feet. The winner flashed a 95 Beyer, and Warlock's Crypt just couldn't keep up. He finished fourth, 10¾ lengths behind. His Beyer went backward to a 68. His cycle was short-circuited.

We all have a favorite trainer or two that we follow. In the mid-Atlantic region, Howard Wolfendale is one of mine. He loves the claiming game and he knows how to play it. When he claims a horse he tries to get the best out of him first time out of the box. These runners generally get bet strongly, and they very often win. He succeeds with an impressive 38 percent first time after the claim.

So, when Fast Jack appeared in the second race at Delaware on October 15, and opened at a surprisingly low 8-5, I gave him a serious look. The field he faced had few really talented runners. But there was a lone speed whose Beyers were improving and who could run figures well up into the 70's under ideal circumstances. And there were a few others who ran consistently in the low-to-mid 70's. Now, Wolfendale is a fine trainer, but the figures for Fast Jack offered very little encouragement. Only once in his recent history had he run above 69—and that was a 73 back on June 16. He had a few chances to repeat or even surpass that Beyer but he had never been able to do it. And Fast Jack was 0 for 14 in 2002—never terribly encouraging. He had run a figure of 72 as a 3-year-old, so the fact that the best he could manage as a 4-year-old was a 73 seemed to indicate that his brief racing career had leveled off somewhere in very mediocre territory. In addition, on July 30 Wolfendale had previously claimed him and waited three weeks before getting Fast Jack to finish a strong second. Unfortunately, he could only raise his Beyer to a 68. All of these were not positive signs. Would this time be any different?

Howard Wolfendale does not fall into the category of "miracle-working" trainers. You can't expect his horses to jump up in spectacular fashion. They may very well improve, but it won't usually be by double-digit Beyers. So, in Fast Jack's case, even if Wolfendale coaxed the best effort out of him, he still appeared overmatched.

On October 15 Fast Jack one-paced it around the Delaware track and ran a very ordinary third. The best he could do was another 69.

---

3 Baeled Haye
Own:Schaefer John & Joanna
Orange, Black Collar, Black Sash, Black
DUNKELBERGER T L (26 4 3 3 .15) 2002:(1043 209 .20)

Ch. g. 3 (Apr)
Sire: Hay Halo (Halo) $2,800
Dam:Count On Baeder(Baederwood)
Br: Marvin Champion (Md)
Tr: Capuano Dale(26 2 5 3 .08) 2002:(822 162 .20)

						Life	6 M 3 1	$11,520 69	D.Fst	5 0 2 1	$8,370 66
						2002	4 M 3 1	$11,520 69	Wet(335)	1 0 1 0	$3,150 69
						2001	2 M 0 0	$0 40	Turf(245)	0 0 0 0	$0 –
				L 121		Lrl	3 0 1 0	$3,780 66	Dst(330)	0 0 0 0	$0 –

9Oct02–2Lrl	fst 6f	:22³ :46² :59 1:11⁴	3+ Md 35000 (40 –35)	66 6 2 2½ 1ʰᵈ 11½ 21½ Dunkelberger T L	L 117 fb	2.40	79 – 19 How'sRaybob115¹½ BeledHye117³¾ DnceAffir117² Speed 2wd, grudgingly 7
27Sep02–10Pim	gd 6f	:23 :46⁴ :59³ 1:13³	3+ Md 25000 (25 –20)	69 6 2 1½ 1½ 1² 21 Dunkelberger T L	L 120 b	3.10	81 – 22 PokerDice115¹ BaeledHaye120³¾ DnceAffir120⁵ Drifted wide, weakened 9
12Sep02–6Pim	fst 6f	:23² :47 :59⁴ 1:13³	3+ Md c– (25 –20)	48 7 4 33½ 35½ 2⁸ 37¾ Fogelsonger R⁵	L 115	6.70	69 – 27 Aldaro120⁶ Dance Affair118¹¾ Baeled Haye115⁵ 3-4wd, empty drive 9
		Claimed from Champion Marvin A for $25,000, Smith Hamilton A Trainer 2002(as of 09/12) : (365 49 47 45 0.13)					
30Aug02–7Tim	fst 4f	:22⁴	:46³ 3+ Md 20000 (25 –20)	57 2 3 3² 2² 2ⁿᵏ Fogelsonger R⁵	L 110	6.30	91 – 14 Jetalito115ⁿᵏ Baeled Haye110³½ Queen's Son114¹ Rallied 8
	Previously trained by Bailes W Robert						
16Dec01–8Lrl	fst 6f	:22³ :46² :59¹ 1:12²	Md 25000 (25 –20)	39 2 2 63¾ 77¼ 8¹⁰ 9¹⁰ Verge M E	120 f	21.60e	67 – 22 Well Pulverized120¾ Noles120¹¾ Georgia Glory111ⁿᵏ Rail, faded 12
28Nov01–8Lrl	fst 6f	:22¹ :46¹ :59 1:12¹	Md Sp Wt 25k	40 9 8 11¹² 11¹² 9¹⁴ 9¹³¾ Verge M E	120 f	88.80	64 – 22 Saints Go Marching120² In The Clear120¾ Root With Style120ⁿᵏ Outrun 12

WORKS: Sep21 Lrl 3f fst :38 Bg 13/17 Sep8 Lrl 4f fst :48³ B 5/15 Aug20 Lrl 4f fst :48² B 4/15 Aug13 Lrl 5f fst 1:04 B 5/5 Aug1 Lrl 5f fst 1:03² Bg 7/12 Jly26 Lrl 5f sly 1:04 B 9/12
TRAINER: Dirt(1537 .23 $1.69) Sprint(1226 .22 $1.66) MdnSpWt(169 .22 $2.09)

The case of Baeled Haye also involves trainer changes and stressful races, but with a somewhat different figure pattern. In the second race at Laurel on October 9, Baeled Haye had the clear top Beyer figure. He had recently been claimed by Maryland's perennial leading trainer, Dale Capuano, and he had immediately responded with a strong effort, dueling the entire trip and jumping up to a lifetime-best figure. How would he react in his next start? Could this top trainer keep the horse from bouncing? Capuano has a long history of sustaining horses at a higher level, and he was moving Baeled Haye up in class, showing confidence that the horse was doing well. Nevertheless, I was still very wary.

On October 9 Baeled Haye ran big. He battled for the lead on the outside, drew off strongly, and was only caught in the last few strides by a very logical closer who had sat a perfect trip. He ran a 66—not bad under such adverse circumstances. Clearly, the role of trainers in figure patterns can complicate matters considerably. But they have to be taken into account before any final judgment can be made.

This is the anatomy of a horse in a gradual decline. You can see it not just in the drops in class, but also in the patterns of Beyers.

A little less than five months ago Swift Knockout was capable of an 87 speed figure, and even after that race in May he was able to cycle back up from 61 to 71 to a winning Beyer of 81. Not surprisingly, he regressed after that hard-fought victory, falling back to a figure of 69. But the race on August 13 provided the first evidence of trouble. Not only did his trainer drop him to a $20,000 claimer, but Swift Knockout was only able to run a 67 at that level. That race was followed by another regression down to a 55, followed by another recovery to Beyers of 67 and 68. There was no evidence of an upward cycle. Instead, there was a repetition of back-to-back Beyers in the upper-60's. Even a further drop to $12,000 couldn't produce a good performance. Swift Knockout had bounced on September 1 after putting together Beyers of 69 and 67. The most recent pairing of 67 and 68 warned of another possible bounce.

On October 17 Swift Knockout was the favorite in a field of six claimers. He sat a perfect trip, waiting behind the speeds on the turn. But when he got clear he had absolutely nothing and faded into the middle of the pack, losing by 5¾ lengths. He fell back again to a 61.

A quick look at the Beyer figures of Amber Comet might lead you to expect a bounce. She looks as if she just ran a "double top" at a high level, and it appears that, in her recent races, she regressed every time she ran a figure in the upper 70's. But a more careful look will raise many doubts about this initial quick impression.

First, in her last six races her two poor Beyers in the 60's were both earned at six furlongs after turning back from two-turn efforts. If you look only at her recent distance races she has Beyers of 77-79-80-80—a remarkably consistent pattern.

Second, she hasn't run in five weeks, which raises the whole controversial question of how much time between races is needed to mitigate any potential bounce. There can be no easy answer to this question. It all depends on the horse. A few might be able to recuperate quickly from an extra-strenuous effort, perhaps needing only two or three weeks. With others four or five weeks might be sufficient. With still others it might take considerably longer. And it also depends on how the horse has been trained in the interim. In the case of Amber Comet, she has one of Maryland's classier trainers, Gary Capuano, who generally handles his horses with good sense and patience. He is not in the habit of rushing horses to the races or running horses that are not ready to give their best.

Amber Comet didn't bounce. In fact, she ran very well on October 17, earning a 78 Beyer, and losing only in the last few strides to the 4-5 favorite, who was on a four-race winning streak. Fortunately, a careful look at Amber Comet's past performances would have saved you the costly embarrassment of throwing her out completely.

2 Nice Boots Baby
Own:Dutrow Anthony W
Black, Red Frogs, Black Cap
ALVARADO F T (37 3 5 5 .08) 2002:(787 91 .12)

Dk. b or br f. 3 (Mar) KEESEP00 $57,000
Sire: Storm Boot (Storm Cat) $15,000
Dam: Foxfire Lass(Premiership)
Br: Richard S Kaster (Ky)
Tr: Dutrow Anthony W(17 7 4 1 .41) 2002:(184 63 .34)

L 116

Life	7	3	1	1	$108,857	93	D.Fst	7	3	1	1	$108,857	93
2002	5	1	1	1	$64,607	93	Wet(310)	0	0	0	0	$0	–
2001	2	2	0	0	$44,250	87	Turf(275)	0	0	0	0	$0	–
Lrl	1	1	0	0	$14,250	86	Dst(345)	7	3	1	1	$108,857	93

9Sep02-7Del	fst	6f		:22^{1}	:45^{2}	:58^{1}	1:10^{3}	3↑ ⒻOClm 50000N	72	2	3	$2^{1\frac{1}{2}}$	2^{hd}	3^{1}	$3^{10\frac{1}{4}}$	Pino M G	L115	1.60	80-14	Ozilda'sKren120^{7} BrelyPerfect115$^{3\frac{1}{4}}$ NiceBootsBby115$^{1\frac{3}{4}}$	Chasd,bid,wknd	6
5Aug02-7Del	fst	6f		:22	:45^{1}	:57^{4}	1:10^{2}	3↑ ⒻOClm 50000N	78	1	1	1^{1}	1^{1}	2^{hd}	$2^{5\frac{3}{4}}$	Pino M G	L114	*.90	85-13	*Ozild'sKren*118$^{5\frac{3}{4}}$ NiceBootsBby114$^{\frac{1}{2}}$ BrelyPerfect116$^{\frac{1}{2}}$	Dueled,saved 2nd	6
13Jly02-10Crc	fst	6f		:21^{3}	:45	:57^{4}	1:10^{4}	ⒻAzalea B C-G3	45	9	3	2^{hd}	2^{hd}	$8^{8\frac{1}{4}}$	$10^{22\frac{1}{4}}$	Pino M G	L116	7.50	68-07	BoldWorld118$^{8\frac{1}{2}}$ WllOnThMov114^{no} TchulMss114^{2}	Bumped st, vied, faded	10
16Feb02-8Aqu	fst	6f	⊡	:22^{3}	:45^{1}	:57^{2}	1:11	ⒻDrlyPrecious80k	57	1	5	$1^{\frac{1}{2}}$	3^{1}	$5^{8\frac{1}{2}}$	$5^{12\frac{1}{4}}$	Pino M G	L122	*.40	77-19	*ProprGmbl*118$^{3\frac{1}{2}}$ DncngBls118^{nk} LostExpcttons116^{nk}	Finished after a half	5
6Jan02-8Aqu	fst	6f	⊡	:23	:47	:58^{3}	1:10^{4}	ⒻRuthless76k	93	2	3	3^{1}	$4^{1\frac{3}{4}}$	$3^{4\frac{1}{2}}$	$1^{2\frac{1}{2}}$	Pino M G	L118	*.95	90-14	NiceBootsBby118$^{2\frac{1}{2}}$ *ProperGmble*118^{nk} AlMxDinr122$^{9\frac{1}{4}}$	Came wide, driving	4
6Dec01-3Aqu	fst	6f	⊡	:22^{2}	:45^{1}	:57^{3}	1:11^{2}	ⒻAlw 50000C	87	1	4	1^{1}	$1^{\frac{1}{2}}$	1^{5}	$1^{3\frac{3}{4}}$	Pino M G	L117	*.65	88-14	*Nice Boots Baby*117$^{3\frac{3}{4}}$ *Vesta*117$^{1\frac{1}{4}}$ Al MaxDiner121$^{\frac{1}{2}}$	Bumped start, driving	5
25Oct01-9Lrl	fst	6f		:21^{4}	:45^{2}	:58	1:11	ⒻMd Sp Wt 25k	86	1	4	1^{3}	1^{2}	1^{5}	$1^{10\frac{3}{4}}$	Pino M G	119	2.40	84-26	*NicBootsBby*119^{10} LdyDiscrt114$^{\frac{3}{4}}$ SonoitSunst119$^{\frac{3}{4}}$	Rail,pace,brisk drive	11

WORKS: Oct22 Lrl 4f fst :49 B *3/19* Oct14 Lrl 4f fst :48^{4} B *7/17* Sep3 Lrl 4f fst :48 B *2/12* ●Aug26 Lrl 4f fst :46^{4} H *1/10* ●Aug17 Lrl 4f fst :48 B *1/49* Jly31 Lrl 4f fst :48 H *2/21*
TRAINER: 31-60Days(97 .32 $1.73) Dirt(395 .34 $1.79) Sprint(256 .32 $1.73) Alw(108 .30 $1.33)

Trainer Anthony Dutrow specializes in developing young horses. His high win percentage reflects a combination of high-quality stock, patient handling, and careful spotting. In the winter of 2001-2002 he had shipped a number of talented youngsters to New York. Most of them ran big races. Nice Boots Baby, for example, turned in two impressive efforts on the inner dirt track before disappointing in the Dearly Precious on February 16.

Nice Boots Baby returned to the races on July 13 at Calder Race

Course after an extensive five-month layoff. She collapsed completely after dueling for the lead. Perhaps this race could be excused: a long layoff, a new track, a tough duel—all could help to explain such a surprisingly poor effort. But there was little excuse for her next race on August 5 at Delaware. Her trip was not difficult in any way, and, most disturbing of all, she could only manage a figure of 78 under such easy conditions—and barely held on to second place after a terrible struggle. In December-January-February, she had run figures of 86-87-93. Now, eight months later, she could only run a 78 in her second start after a layoff. Young horses should show natural improvement in their Beyers in the transition from 2 to 3 years old. If they don't show the normal progress that comes with physical maturation—if they should even regress in their figures—that's not a good sign. Perhaps you could argue that Nice Boots Baby was gradually coming back after the layoff with improving Beyers of 45 to 78, but she still had a long way to go to even approach her 2-year-old numbers, and she simply did not look like the same powerful animal that had shipped up to Aqueduct the previous winter.

On September 9 at Delaware she chased the pace in the two path and began to fade even before they reached the top of the stretch. She simply could not keep up. Something was seriously amiss with Nice Boots Baby. Her Beyer figures had signaled it. But her early reputation continued to attract big money. Even after her two poor performances she still went off at a very short price. In this case, the figures showed that she no longer deserved the reputation that had lingered from her exciting races way back in the winter.

3 Shake A Leg
Own: Dutrow Anthony W
Black, Red Frogs, Black Cap
PINO M G (28 8 4 1 .29) 2002:(1184 253 .21)

B. f. 2 (Mar) OBSAPR02 $57,000
Sire: Gold Alert (Mr. Prospector) $4,000
Dam: Danzalot Miss (Premiership)
Br: John Franks (Fla)
Tr: Dutrow Anthony W (6 3 1 0 .50) 2002:(170 58 .34)

L 122

Life	2 M	1 0	$12,770	63	D.Fst	2 0 1 0	$12,770	63
2002	2 M	1 0	$12,770	63	Wet(320)	0 0 0 0	$0	–
2001	0 M	0 0	$0	–	Turf(225)	0 0 0 0	$0	–
Lrl	0 0	0 0	$0	–	Dst(335)	1 0 1 0	$11,600	63

30Sep02-6Del fst 5½f :21⁴ :46¹ :59³ 1:06¹ ⓕMd Sp Wt 40k 50 8 2 2¼ 2hd 22½ 55 Pino M G L 120 *.90 81–17 BorderBound120²¼ BlzingTun120hd SwingingBrz120²¼ Couldn't sustain bid 9
7Sep02-1Del fst 6f :22 :45⁴ :59³ 1:13² ⓕMd Sp Wt 59k 63 8 2 2¼ 1hd 11½ 2no Black A S L 120 2.30 76–17 FollowTheQueen120no ShkALg120² SwingingBrz120½ Clear, couldn't last 10
WORKS: ●Oct14 Lrl 4f fst :47³ H 1/17 ●Sep25 Lrl 4f fst :48 H 1/26 ●Sep4 Lrl 3f fst :36 Bg 1/7 Aug29 Lrl 5f sly 1:01⁴ H 3/6 ●Aug19 Lrl 4f fst :48 B 1/7 Aug12 Lrl 4f fst :47⁴ H 2/6
TRAINER: 2YO(90 .36 $2.08) Dirt(381 .34 $1.78) Sprint(246 .31 $1.73) MdnSpWt(84 .35 $2.03)

Is this a promising young 2-year-old? Or a horse ready to bounce? Or both? The answer is, in most such cases, both.

Shake A Leg's first race showed that she had talent, but it was a hard effort for a debut runner, and could certainly have taken something out of this filly. A horse like Shake A Leg will always be over-bet in her second start, as Shake A Leg was at less than even money. But, since an inexperienced, immature young filly might need a little time to recover from such a strenuous effort, you should not hesitate to bet against these severe underlays. Paradoxically, in many of these cases, the more impressive the Beyer in that first race under strenuous circumstances, the more likely that the horse will run worse in her second start.

In the case of Shake A Leg, she ran fifth in her next race, with a Beyer of only 50. Of course, there are horses with this kind of big debut effort that will run well next time out, especially if they have sufficient time between races. But they always have one thing in common: They are inordinately short prices and worth taking a shot against.

Connemara opened on the tote board at odds of 1-5, and you can understand why. His form looked overwhelming, with his last two figures towering over nearly all his rivals, and the field he faced was unusually weak. But Connemara's past performances flashed more caution lights than a railway signal at rush hour.

First, he was a 5-year-old maiden with frequent and lengthy gaps in his form. Clearly this was a horse with some physical problems—the kind of horse you don't want to risk playing under any circumstances, especially at a ridiculously short price.

Second, while he ran a relatively unstressful race on July 23 after a long layoff, his second race had to be an exhausting effort, dueling through the entire six furlongs and losing out by a head in the final strides. That was an all-out, lifetime-best effort that had to take its toll, especially on a physically questionable 5-year-old.

Third, his trainer had rushed him back in 14 days after his first race. That's a lot to ask from an unsound, modestly talented horse. With so little time to recuperate between races, a reaction becomes much more likely.

Fourth, there was at least one other speed horse to harass Connemara, so he couldn't expect to get an easy, loose-on-the-lead trip.

Connemara's past performances should have been accompanied by a warning label, or perhaps a skull and crossbones denoting "POISON." Actually, it could have been worse. Connemara didn't run all that terribly, but he could only manage a well-beaten second. His Beyer dropped to 49.

If you're looking for a Beyer figure cycle, Mahogany Ship's form seems to fit the parameters to perfection. But a closer study raises some serious doubts.

Mahogany Ship returned from a two-month layoff to run a lifetime-best Beyer of 83 on May 5. Then, quite predictably, he retreated down to a 66 over his next two starts. He followed that race with an improved effort, so his figure could logically be projected to return to the low 80's in his next start—except for three elements that disturbed me.

First, Mahogany Ship had not won a race in two years, but that was only a minor, if nagging, problem.

Second, the trainer was dropping him down to a $16,000 claimer after the horse ran a very strong effort for $25,000, and Mahogany Ship had not run now in four weeks. Was there something wrong physically? Or was the trainer simply looking to end the frustration and finally win a race with this perpetual bridesmaid?

Third, you had to ask yourself: Was it realistic to expect Mahogany Ship to improve again to an 83? Was that May 5 race a reliable measure of his potential? After all, he had earned that 83 Beyer under the most ideal circumstances, opening an easy, uncontested lead on a speed-favoring track. Under today's less than ideal conditions (there were plenty of other speed horses in this race), could Mahogany Ship reproduce a figure of 83?

Actually, a move all the way up to an 83 probably would not be necessary in the field he faced. Few of the other contenders had shown a capacity to run much above the mid-70's. So Mahogany Ship was probably still a good bet, although I could certainly understand a player being scared off by all those second- and third-place finishes in his record. As it turned out, Mahogany Ship only improved to a Beyer of 78, but he won by 1¾ lengths.

7 February Storm
Own: The Thoroughbred Corp
Green And White Stripes; Green Cap.
BOREL C H (1 0 0 0 .00) 2002:(961 133 .14)

B. c. 3 (Apr)
Sire: Storm Cat (Storm Bird) $500,000
Dam: Lilac Garden(Roberto)
Br: The Thoroughbred Corp (Ky)
Tr: Lukas D Wayne(1 0 1 0 .00) 2002:(360 64 .18)

L 117

Life	15	3	2	2	$139,385	91	D.Fst	3	0	0	0	$0	75
2002	12	3	1	2	$131,785	91	Wet(345)	1	0	0	0	$3,000	79
2001	3	M	1	0	$7,600	80	Turf(330)	11	3	2	2	$136,385	91
Kee Ⓣ	0	0	0	0	$0	–	Dst Ⓣ (340)	5	2	1	1	$74,060	90

31Aug02-7Sar	gd	1	(T) :24 :473 1:122 1:372	3↑ Alw 50000N3L	86	7	21½	2½	1½	1½	11¾	Chavez J F	L 117 b	3.60	81-20	February Storm1171¾ Charioteer117no Gasperillo Daze121nk	Dug in gamely	9
17Aug02-7Sar	gd	1⅛	⊗ :473 1:121 1:383 1:522	3↑ Alw 50000N2X	79	1	11½	1½	1½	42	45	Chavez J F	L 117 b	5.80	72-19	Hitchin' Post121hd Cardiff Arms1163¼ Marhoob1211½	Set pace, tired	8
3Aug02-10Sar	sf	1	(T) :242 :481 1:122 1:364	3↑ Alw 50000N2X	86	4	23	21½	21½	34	35¼	Chavez J F	L 117 b	3.60	79-24	*RiverRush*1213½ YnkeeGntlmn1171¾ FbruryStorm117no	With pace, no rally	9
29Jun02-8AP	fm	1 1/16	Ⓣ :232 :473 1:113 1:414	Arl Classic-G2	85	4	32½	31	31	62¾	83½	Sibille R	L 116 b	11.80	97-07	Mr. Mellon121nk Doc Holiday1211¾ Seainsky116nk	3 wide, tired	9
8Jun02-9CD	fm	1⅛	Ⓣ :463 1:11 1:361 1:482	JeffersonCupG3	78	5	51¼	46½	32	3½	46¾	Borel C H	L 115 b	4.60	87-10	*Orchard Park*1191 *Mr. Mellon*1122½ Quest Star1133¼	5w,stalk,flatten out	8
18May02-5Pim	yl	1 1/16	Ⓣ :24 :492 1:143 1:46	Woodlawn75k	85	5	76½	54	42	32½	34	Espinoza V	L 117 b	*1.70	69-26	Mr.O'brien1152½ ReglSnction1151½ FbruryStorm117½	4wd turns, mild rally	8
27Apr02-7Hol	fm	1 1/16	Ⓣ :242 :481 1:122 1:42	Alw 51000N1X	91	7	52½	52½	52½	2hd	12	Espinoza V	LB 122 b	3.40	85-15	February Storm1222 Greenhills120no *Sunkosi*120½	Pulled,4wd bid,clear	10
6Apr02-2SA	fm	1	Ⓣ :231 :473 1:12 1:36	Md Sp Wt 50k	90	3	54	41½	3½	11	1¾	Espinoza V	LB 120 b	5.10	82-15	*FbruryStorm*120¾ PrincDumni120nk *Chislling*1201½	3wd bid,led,held game	11
9Mar02-7GG	fst	1 1/16	- :224 :462 1:102 1:432	ElCaminoDby-G3	75	6	44	52½	54¼	65½	67	Pedroza M A	LB 116 b	34.80	79-17	Yougottwnn120¾ Dnthebluegrssmn1172 LustyLtin1151½	Stlkd rail, wknd	10
24Feb02-1SA	fm	1⅛	Ⓣ :47 1:111 1:354 1:474	Md Sp Wt 48k	78	5	31½	33	31	21	2nk	Espinoza V	LB 120 b	1.50e	90-10	*Johar*120nk February Storm120½ Van Rouge1205½	Bid,game btwn late	7
6Feb02-4SA	fm	*6½f	Ⓣ :223 :454 1:084 1:143	Md Sp Wt 46k	77	7	5	42½	51¾	41¼	63¾	Baze T C	LB 120 b	15.90	80-16	*Royal Gem*1201½ Golden Arrow1201 Hecandigit120nk	Btwn foes,rail bid str	10
17Jan02-4SA	fm	1	Ⓣ :223 :463 1:114 1:354	Md Sp Wt 48k	73	4	53	53¾	62¾	54	57½	Espinoza V	LB 120 b	*1.10	75-17	Easy Grades1203 Chiselling1202 Mister G. Q.1201	Pulld btwn,no late bid	10

WORKS: Sep29 Bel 4f fst :484 B *30/69* Sep21 Bel 4f fst :492 B *26/51* Sep15 Bel 4f fst :491 B *8/42* Sep9 Bel 4f fst :483 B *6/26* Aug13 Sar tr.t 4f fst :504 B *3/14* Jly28 Sar tr.t 5f fst 1:024 B *5/14*
TRAINER: 31-60Days(192 .19 $1.69) Turf(119 .14 $1.35) Stakes(65 .20 $2.17)

This example is a bit of a stretch. You have to dig rather deeper than with most other cases. But the thinking behind it can be used to uncover other well-hidden runners at good prices. After all, without a little camouflage in the past performances, it's hard to get a price.

Back in California in the spring, February Storm had put together back-to-back lifetime bests of 90 and 91 on the turf. D. Wayne Lukas then took the colt on the road for a minor stakes tour. Not surprisingly, the two big Beyers—in addition to some tough trips and off-turf conditions—set him back for a while. He began to rebound with his 85 figure in the Arlington Classic. From there you might have expected significant further improvement. But in the race on August 3 at Saratoga, February Storm had no chance at all. The jockeys had allowed River Rush to waltz along solo on a ridiculously slow pace, with February Storm reluctantly taking up the chase. Whether it was due to the impossible circumstances or the soft turf, February Storm ran a Beyer of only 86. Excusable, but still not terribly encouraging.

Two weeks later, February Storm's next race was taken off the grass. But Lukas ran him anyway. You don't pass up many dances when you're a resident in the D. Wayne Lukas barn. To no one's surprise, February Storm ran poorly. Then, precisely two weeks after that, on August 31, he returned again to the turf— now with recent form that, at least superficially, did not look all that inviting. But the potential clearly was there in this young 3-year-old, as his best California races had shown. His condition was not in question since he had been running regularly and he had been plagued by difficult trips and unfavorable conditions in his last two races. If he could once again run a figure in the 90 range, or even higher, he would have today's field pretty much at his mercy. Even a Beyer in the high 80's would probably win in this less than stellar allowance race.

February Storm chased and dueled from an outside post, and prevailed by $1\sqrt[3]{4}$ lengths in a game effort. He paid $9.20.

February Storm required a somewhat more imaginative use of the Beyer figures, a more in-depth backward look through the past performances, and a knowledge of the circumstances of the River Rush race on August 3. And it required a slight leap of faith. Perhaps the price could have been better, but you were rewarded with a courageous, high-caliber performance by a developing young turf horse.

7 Mr Notebook
Own:Pattituci Florence
Blue, Red And White Stripes, White Stars **$45,000**
ZAMORA T A (113 8 8 11 .07) 2002:(119 8 .07)

Ch. c. 4 (May)
Sire: Notebook (Well Decorated) $15,000
Dam:Raahia(Vice Regent)
Br: Herman Heinlein (Fla)
Tr: Benson Harry(16 1 2 0 .06) 2002:(41 2 .05)

L 116

Life	30	5	2	3	$197,480	94	**D.Fst**	5	1	0	0	$19,100	81
2002	8	1	0	0	$27,670	94	**Wet(400)**	3	1	0	0	$16,760	73
2001	15	0	2	3	$53,620	94	**Turf(240)**	22	3	2	3	$161,620	94
Del Ⓣ	5	1	0	0	$28,380	94	**DstⓉ(330)**	15	3	0	1	$117,821	94

25Sep02-9Del	fm	$1\frac{1}{16}$	Ⓣ	$:23^{2}$	$:47$	$1:11^{1}$	$1:42^{3}$	3↑ Clm 25000(25-20)	**94**	6	1^{hd}	1^{2}	1^{2}	1^{5}	$1^{1\frac{1}{2}}$	Zamora T A	L118 b	35.90	94-09	MrNotebook$118^{1\frac{1}{2}}$ SpecialDncer118^{4} Hllucinogin$118^{1\frac{1}{2}}$	Drew off, prevailed	12
11Aug02-5Mth	fm	$1\frac{1}{16}$	Ⓣ	$:23^{2}$	$:47$	$1:11^{1}$	$1:42^{1}$+	3↑ Clm 25000(25-20)	**69**	6	3^{3}	3^{5}	$4^{2\frac{3}{4}}$	$7^{6\frac{1}{4}}$	8^{9}	Velez J A Jr	L116	10.10	81-16	Reason To Squall$116^{3\frac{1}{2}}$ *Monet*$116^{1\frac{1}{2}}$ Highgain115^{nk}	Good position, tired	9
22Jly02-8Del	fm	$1\frac{1}{16}$	Ⓣ	$:23^{1}$	$:47^{2}$	$1:11^{4}$	$1:43^{2}$	3↑ Clm 50000(50-45)	**74**	10	3^{5}	4^{3}	$5^{4\frac{3}{4}}$	$7^{6\frac{3}{4}}$	7^{8}	Castillo O O	L118	43.00	82-10	*Stauch*$118^{2\frac{1}{2}}$ Cynics Beware$118^{1\frac{1}{2}}$ Pavillon$120^{\frac{3}{4}}$	Lacked a rally	10
18Jun02-8Del	gd	$*1\frac{1}{16}$	Ⓣ	$:25$	$:49^{4}$	$1:14^{3}$	$1:47^{1}$	3↑ Clm 60000(60-50)	**41**	8	1^{hd}	1^{hd}	2^{hd}	9^{11}	10^{23}	Castillo O O	L118	11.00	55-22	Pavillon$118^{1\frac{1}{4}}$ Full Brush118^{nk} Nordagus116^{1}	Vied 2 wide, faltered	10
4Jun02-8Del	fm	1	Ⓣ	$:23^{2}$	$:46^{3}$	$1:10^{4}$	$1:35^{1}$	3↑ Clm 60000(60-50)	**86**	5	5^{9}	6^{10}	5^{10}	$4^{8\frac{1}{2}}$	$4^{6\frac{3}{4}}$	Dominguez R A	L118	4.90	93 —	*TwilightPrince*$120^{5\frac{3}{4}}$ Roberto'sPrid116^{1} *CstlComr*116no	Lacked solid rally	8
3Mar02-7GP	fm	1	Ⓣ	$:22^{3}$	$:46$	$1:10$	$1:35^{4}$	4↑ Clm 75000(75-65)	**55**	1	7^{14}	7^{14}	10^{15}	10^{12}	10^{19}	Santos J A	L120	11.60	68-12	*Wertz*$120^{1\frac{3}{4}}$ Slowhand$119^{1\frac{3}{4}}$ Gail's Drive$120^{1\frac{1}{2}}$	Outrun	11
1Feb02-9GP	sly	1^{70}	⊗	$:24^{1}$	$:49$	$1:14^{1}$	$1:45$	4↑ Alw 46000N$mY	**69**	3	2^{3}	2^{4}	$5^{4\frac{1}{4}}$	$5^{6\frac{1}{2}}$	4^{12}	Santos J A	L116 f	6.40	64-34	Flying Avie$120^{2\frac{1}{2}}$ Royal Romp$116^{1\frac{1}{4}}$ Sejm's Madness$122^{8\frac{1}{4}}$	Chased, tired	5
12Jan02-10GP	fm	$*1\frac{1}{16}$	Ⓣ	$:24^{1}$	$:49^{2}$	$1:14$	$1:45^{1}$+	4↑ OClm 100000(100-90)N	**87**	8	$2^{1\frac{1}{2}}$	2^{2}	$2^{1\frac{1}{2}}$	3^{3}	6^{6}	Rivera J A II	L120	34.80	72-23	Drama Critic$120^{2\frac{1}{4}}$ Scagnelli$118^{\frac{1}{2}}$ *In Frank's Honor*$120^{1\frac{1}{2}}$	Chased, tired	10
Previously trained by Alonso Enrique																						
13Dec01-9Crc	gd	1	Ⓣ	$:23^{3}$	$:48$	$1:11^{1}$	$1:35^{3}$	3↑ OClm 62500(62.5-57.5)N	**94**	8	3^{1}	$2^{\frac{1}{2}}$	2^{hd}	1^{1}	$2^{\frac{1}{2}}$	Rivera J A II	L114	17.70	89-18	*Pisces*$117^{\frac{1}{2}}$ Mr Notebook$114^{1\frac{1}{4}}$ LouisianaAllen119^{nk}	Slim lead, outfinished	8
24Nov01-10Crc	fm	$1\frac{1}{16}$	Ⓣ	$:22^{4}$	$:46^{3}$	$1:09^{4}$	$1:40^{2}$	The Vid H60k	**81**	8	$2^{\frac{1}{2}}$	2^{1}	$2^{1\frac{1}{2}}$	$5^{5\frac{1}{2}}$	$8^{8\frac{1}{2}}$	Ramgeet A R	L121	38.50	86-07	TorOfThCt$116^{\frac{1}{2}}$ TvSportsDrctor$118^{3\frac{1}{4}}$ Vkdonts118^{hd}	Prompted, gave way	12

WORKS: **Sep18 Del 4f fst $:50^{2}$ B** *28/56* **Sep9 Del 5f fst $1:03^{3}$ Bg** *9/18*
TRAINER: Turf(26 .15 $3.71) Routes(41 .15 $3.33) Claim(49 .08 $2.71)

The ninth race at Delaware on September 25 was a real mind-bender, attracting a full field of 12 on the grass at $1\frac{1}{16}$ miles. A quick inventory of the Beyer figures showed that seven of the horses looked like they could run in the mid-to-upper 80's. The other five simply did not measure up. They could be safely eliminated. Of course, that still left more than half the field with live chances.

Out of the seven contenders, perhaps the most intriguing was Mr Notebook. His owner seemed reluctant to part with him, and so continued to run him at the $50,000-$60,000 level where he clearly could no longer compete very profitably. He had run a solid 86 Beyer on June 4 after a three-month layoff, but that had only earned him a distant fourth-place finish. He appeared to be cycling back to a race in the mid 80's when his connections, in an intelligent if belated acceptance of reality, shipped him to Monmouth and dropped him down to $25,000. He did absolutely nothing. Perhaps he hated Monmouth. Perhaps he shipped poorly. Or perhaps he was just finished. There was really no way to tell.

Six weeks later Mr Notebook reappeared at Delaware in another $25,000 claimer, this time with blinkers added. If you were willing to excuse that one poor effort at Monmouth, if you were willing to give him one more chance to return to that Beyer of 86, if you were willing to add him to the mix in this contentious race on September 25, you were richly rewarded at odds of 35-1. He won by 1½ lengths and soared to a figure of 94.

If you like to spread around in pick threes or pick fours or pick sixes, a horse like Mr Notebook can make your ticket. You certainly couldn't stand alone with him, but a deeper, more creative look at his Beyer figures might at least lead you to use him along with other more obviously logical types. With a little luck a horse like Mr Notebook could even make your meet.

3c Wonderful Larry
Own: Tradewinds Stable
Red, Black And White Sash
$16,000
MUNAR L H (25 7 4 3 .28) 2002:(564 93 .16)

Ch. g. 6
Sire: Compelling Sound (Seattle Slew) $2,500
Dam: Luscious Linda (Strawberry Road*Aus)
Br: Jones John F Jr & Lippert Marshall (Ky)
Tr: Zimmerman John C(31 5 6 2 .16) 2002:(447 112 .25)

L 120

Life	41	14	5	5	$226,411	102	D.Fst	38	11	5	5	$198,256	102
2002	8	3	1	1	$46,790	88	Wet(325)	3	3	0	0	$28,155	88
2001	6	1	1	1	$17,086	89	Turf(255)	0	0	0	0	$0	–
Del	9	4	1	1	$82,850	99	Dst(310)	26	11	4	4	$178,920	102

7Oct02-8Del	fst	6f	:214	:451	:58	1:11	3↑ Clm 16000 (16-14)	86	5	3	1 1½	12½	14	12½	Munar L H	L 120 fb	4.60	88-17	WondrfulLrry1202½ LvItToBzr120nk Trvor'sLuckyOn1181¾	Steady pressure	7
18Sep02-2Med	fst	6f	:214	:451	:574	1:103	3↑ Clm 20000 (20-18)	58	1	9	84½	88¼	95¾	712	Mojica R Jr	L 119 fb	4.90	74-20	KohunaGrnde116hd *AllTheMrbles*1196 Pulitzer1161¼	No speed,drifted out	9
15Aug02-7Pen	sly	6f	:211	:433	:564	1:101	3↑ OClm 20000	79	2	1	11	13	16	13½	Munar L H	L 116 fb	3.30	94-10	Wonderful Larry1163½ Pulitzer116¾ Graceful Devil119¾	2 wide, driving	5
11Aug02-8Del	fst	6f	:223	:453	:574	1:11	3↑ Clm 25000 (25-20)	64	3	4	41½	66¾	69	79¼	Castillo O O	L 118 fb	7.20	79-15	**Golden O's**118½ Love Happy1181¾ Whatshisname1203	Prompted, tired	8
20Jly02-2Mth	gd	6f	:222	:452	:573	1:102	3↑ Clm 16000 (16-14)	88	4	3	2½	2hd	11	11¾	Mojica R Jr	L 116 fb	3.90	87-15	WonderfulLrry1161¾ Musshi1081¼ Mr.UnitedStts1151	Edged clear,driving	9
30Jun02-9Del	fst	6f	:221	:452	:582	1:114	3↑ Clm 25000 (25-20)	66	2	8	73¾	75¾	76	87¼	Flores E	L 118 fb	5.50	77-20	Whatshisnme120nk ProspectMrk118½ PotomcCity118no	Failed to menace	9
1Jun02-4Pim	fst	6f	:23	:46	:583	1:12	4↑ Clm 25000 (25-20)	81	6	3	2½	2hd	13½	31	Flores E	L 117 fb	5.70	84-12	SrtogBrodwy117nk Lk'sWy119¾ WndrflLrry117½	3wd,drifted out,weaknd	6
20May02-5Del	fst	6f	:214	:453	:583	1:112	3↑ Clm 25000 (25-20)	67	5	4	51½	61¾	38	28¾	Acosta J D5	L 111 fb	*2.10	77-17	*LoveHppy*1168¾ WonderfulLrry111nk HighAbove116½	Shuffled, up for 2nd	7
8Apr01-3Del	fst	6f	:213	:444	:574	1:102	4↑ Clm 25000 (25-22.5)	78	4	2	31	3nk	1hd	35¼	McCarthy M J	L 118 fb	2.30	86-13	Mount Green1183½ Nazca1181¾ Wonderful Larry1183	3 wide bid, faded	6
10Mar01-6Pen	fst	5½f	:214	:451	:58	1:043	4↑ Alw 16864N$Y	75	2	5	2hd	1hd	12	42	Munar L H	L 116 fb	2.50	91-18	*BohemiSlew*1161½ AdmsGoldNuggtt116½ PtchnsRosBowl116no	Weakened	7

TRAINER: Dirt(924 .25 $2.19) Sprint(623 .26 $2.05) Claim(699 .24 $2.11)

Success stories like that of Mr Notebook don't happen every day. But they are not all that unusual, either. At Delaware Park on October 7, for example, Wonderful Larry had a somewhat similar pattern. He had run a huge race back on July 20 at Monmouth for a $16,000 claiming tag—a Beyer of 88, which would very likely win the Delaware race. He had gone through the typical bounce and recovery until he was sent to The Meadowlands, where he didn't do any running at all. The race could easily be excused. Wonderful Larry certainly wouldn't be the first horse to run badly first time under the lights, and the fact that he showed none of his usual speed suggests just such a negative response. As with Mr Notebook, if you were willing to set aside one disastrous race, Wonderful Larry was very playable in his return to the $16,000 level.

At Delaware, Wonderful Larry hustled to the lead, led every step of the way, and won off by 2½ lengths. He paid $11.20. His Beyer cycled back to an 86.

The form of Halo World is not typical. Far from it. A horse who can improve his Beyer figures for seven consecutive races is very rare indeed. To do it as a 7-year-old is even rarer still. You can look for explanations: Very gradual improvement in his figures mitigated against any bounce; changes in trainers helped keep him fresh; his races were sensibly spaced, his placement equally sensible and unambitious. But you can't really account for such unusual, uninterrupted development. There will always be the occasional horse like Halo World who violates all the conventional guidelines. You keep betting against them, and they just keep getting better. Fortunately, there aren't too many like Halo World.

Finally, on October 8 Halo World stopped his seemingly endless escalation. But he only fell back a few points, and he almost won the race anyway.

1 Cuban Link
Own: Pink Toes Farm
Navy Blue, White Diamond Belt, White **$15,000**
DUARTE J C JR (379 50 52 49 .13) 2002:(439 56 .13)

Dk. b or br c. 3 (Mar) EASMAY01 $19,000
Sire: Mr. Greeley (Gone West) $25,000
Dam: Helenas' Surprise(Marfa)
Br: Brent Harris (Ky)
Tr: Curry Dee(112 20 8 18 .18) 2002:(128 21 .16)

L 122

Life	5	2	0	0	$13,740	73	**D.Fst**	4	1	0	0	$7,740 73
2002	5	2	0	0	$13,740	73	**Wet(380)**	1	1	0	0	$6,000 72
2001	0	M	0	0	$0	–	**Turf(290)**	0	0	0	0	$0 –
Pha	4	2	0	0	$13,440	73	**Dst(355)**	2	0	0	0	$1,440 54

1Oct02-3Pha	fst	$5\frac{1}{2}$f	:22	$:45^1$	$:57^4$	$1{:}04^3$	Clm 10000N2L	**73**	6	5	3^1	$2^{1\frac{1}{2}}$	$1^{\frac{1}{2}}$	1^4	Pena A	L 122 fb	2.00	90–13	Cuban Link122^4 Juramento$113^{5\frac{1}{4}}$ Daddy Grace120^{no}	3 wide move,drew off	7
16Sep02-3Pha	sly	$5\frac{1}{2}$f	$:22^1$	$:46^2$	$:58^3$	1:05	3↑ Md 15000(15–13)	**72**	4	1	2^1	$2^{1\frac{1}{2}}$	$1^{1\frac{1}{2}}$	1^4	Pena A	L 118 fb	*1.50	88–19	*CubnLink*118^4 DingoRngo$118^{4\frac{3}{4}}$ SlorsHornpp$122^{2\frac{1}{2}}$	Stalked,bid4w,drew off	6
25Aug02-9Pha	fst	7f	$:22^3$	$:46^1$	1:12	$1{:}25^2$	3↑ Md 25000(25–20)	**52**	11	2	$4^{2\frac{1}{2}}$	$3^{2\frac{1}{2}}$	$2^{2\frac{1}{2}}$	$6^{9\frac{1}{2}}$	Espindola M A	119 fb	9.50	66–24	Fugitivo$118^{1\frac{1}{2}}$ The Other Me116^3 Our Louie118^3	Stalked 3 wide, empty	11
10Aug02-8Del	fst	6f	$:22^2$	$:45^4$	$:58^2$	$1{:}11^3$	3↑ Md Sp Wt 39k	**38**	5	5	2^1	$8^{7\frac{1}{2}}$	8^{12}	9^{16}	Espindola M A	119 fb	22.30	69–21	Glint$119^{\frac{3}{4}}$ Crossing Creek$119^{3\frac{3}{4}}$ Quietamericanforce$119^{2\frac{1}{2}}$	Faltered	9
21Jly02-9Pha	fst	6f	$:21^4$	$:44^4$	$:57^1$	$1{:}10^2$	Md Sp Wt 21k	**54**	7	10	$9^{5\frac{1}{4}}$	6^5	4^6	$4^{7\frac{1}{4}}$	Espindola M A	122 fb	15.20	80–14	Look Lively$122^{1\frac{1}{4}}$ In Need Of Reign122^2 Fugitivo122^4	Inside, no factor	11

TRAINER: Dirt(285 .14 $1.68) Sprint(213 .15 $1.65) Claim(179 .13 $1.33)

Finally, there's the case of Cuban Link. It falls in the "closing the gap" department. In the third race at Philadelphia Park on September 16 he had won his maiden with a big Beyer figure of 72. In his next race on October 1 he faced six competitors whose last-race Beyers were 52, 46, 40, 36, 26, and 16—twenty points or more behind the top figure. Even if Cuban Link ran much slower this time, could anyone close such a huge gap? My answer would have been an emphatic "I don't know about that, but I wouldn't want to bet Cuban Link no matter what." After all, Cuban Link was a cheap maiden claimer. He had won his maiden on a sloppy track, and on first-time Lasix. And now he was facing winners for the first time—although an admittedly sorry bunch of winners. A big reaction could be anticipated for Cuban Link. His Beyer pattern cried out "bounce," "three-and-out," or whatever.

On October 1 Cuban Link won again, with ease, by four lengths. He ran another solid Beyer of 73.

It's just a reminder that they don't always bounce the way they're supposed to. In fact, they don't do *anything* every time the way they're supposed to. Which is only another way of saying, "Don't ever get the idea that this is an easy game."

7

CONCLUSION: BEYER LIMITS

THE BEYER SPEED Figures are a powerful tool. But there are some things even the Beyer figures can't help you with—most especially, the two main obstacles in the way of the winning horseplayer. I'm talking about jockey error and bettor brain-lock.

Take the fifth race at Philadelphia on October 22. In this complicated affair, Henbane Man looked like he could be cycling back up to a Beyer figure in the upper 60's. That could very well be enough to put him first or second in this seven-horse field of limited claimers. That was the good news. The bad news, at least potentially, was his rider: a five-pound apprentice with a 6 percent win rate at the meeting. But that, in turn, was counteracted by the best news of all, the price: Henbane Man was 16-1.

As the field raced into the first turn, Henbane Man settled comfortably in last. No surprise there. But as soon as they straightened out on the backstretch I was surprised to see a horse rushing up furiously on the outside. It was Henbane Man. The apprentice appeared to have some sort of sudden inspiration, as if he had just remembered something important he had to do, or perhaps he mistook the backstretch for the real stretch. He had yanked his horse out into the five path and pressed on the accelerator, rushing Henbane Man past the entire field. Before they reached the far turn he was actually challenging for the lead. He even took over the lead in upper stretch. But you could see the bad news coming.

As his premature efforts began to take their toll, Henbane Man was passed very late by one of the logical closers. Not to worry. There were still the exactas to root for. When another horse wore him down even later in the stretch, there were still the trifectas to fall back on. When he was finally nosed out right on the wire for third place, the disaster was complete. Henbane Man, probably best, lost by $2^{1}/_{4}$ lengths. Thanks to a spectacularly misjudged ride, his Beyer had only improved to a 65 and that knocked him completely out of the money.

The Beyer Speed Figures had come up with a very live 16-1 shot. But the Beyer figures can't teach jockeys how to ride, or prevent them from the kind of mind-boggling incompetence that sabotaged Henbane Man's chances.

We've seen how an imaginative use of speed figures can uncover big opportunities—even in the most unpromising-looking places. Such was the case in the second race at Delaware on October 23.

Eleven talent-challenged fillies went to the post in this $12,500 maiden claimer. Many players groan when they see such fields, and hurry to skip over them. But that can sometimes prove to be a costly bit of snobbery. In this case, the presence of a horse like Fillypasser pulled me in deeper in search of a major score. One look at the tote board and you quickly forgot about the poverty of talent in this field.

If your horse could run six furlongs with a Beyer in the mid-40's, you were a strong contender in this event. Still, even with this rather minimal threshhold, there were at least four or five fillies who could not hope to reach that level. Even a figure in the 30's looked well beyond them. Another filly looked borderline, but I decided to eliminate her as well because she had been laid off for 3½ months, was being dropped down severely, and was running a distance that looked much too short for her. That left only five possibilities, with Fillypasser as the key.

8 Fillypasser
Own: The Elkstone Group
White, Orange 'e', Elkhead On Lime Ball, **$20,000**
UMANA J L (502 44 65 75 .09) 2002:(932 94 .10)

Dk. b or br f. 3 (Feb)
Sire: Prospector's Halo (Gold Stage)
Dam: Lin D. Time (Manifesto)
Br: Scott Dudley (Fla)
Tr: Stauffer Arthur F(57 2 3 6 .04) 2002:(62 3 .05)

L 115

Life	11	1	2	3	$23,270	51	
2002	11	1	2	3	$23,270	51	
2001	0	M	0	0	$0	–	
Del	6	1	0	2	$14,370	49	
D.Fst	10	1	2	3	$23,020	51	
Wet(325)	1	0	0	0	$250	32	
Turf(165*)	0	0	0	0	$0	–	
Dst(330)	9	1	2	2	$20,040	51	

23Oct02-2Del fst 6f :223 :473 1:012 1:141 3↑ Ⓕ Md 12500 (12.5-10.5) **45** 8 9 52 32½ 1½ 16 Umana J L L 120 b 21.70 72-13 Fillypasser1206 Fennel120½ Little Wilder120½ 3 wide bid, drew off 11
2Oct02-9Del fst 5f :214 :46 :592 3↑ Ⓕ Md 12500 (12.5-10.5) **18** 3 10 1112 910 815 512½ Umana J L L 120 b 13.70 76-14 CllMeChiffie1205¾ MuiMdness1184½ AbsentAshle123nk Passed tiring rivals 11
15Sep02-4Del wf 6f :23 :48 1:011 1:152 3↑ Ⓕ Md 16000 (16-14) **32** 7 7 41½ 84¾ 65 75½ Rose J L 120 b 5.80 60-30 Man In Blue120no Absent Ashlee1211½ Delayed Ride1181½ Showed little 8
21Aug02-2Del fst 6f :224 :471 1:002 1:132 3↑ Ⓕ Md 25000 (25-20) **19** 4 9 95¼ 89 712 617¾ Rose J L 119 b 5.80 58-19 SllyGotTheBoot1191¼ **GloriousTun**1197 Hlo'sSugr119½ Failed to menace 9
6Aug02-5Del fst 6f :231 :474 1:002 1:132 3↑ Ⓕ Md 20000 (25-20) **49** 6 7 78½ 68 48½ 36½ McCarthy M J L 117 b 4.60 69-21 Blend Of Devil1194 ***Starvest***1232½ Fillypasser1173 Mild late rally 7
10Jly02-3Del fst 6f :223 :472 1:002 1:13 3↑ Ⓕ Md c-(12.5-10.5) **44** 2 7 52¾ 64 55 38½ Dominguez R A L 118 b *.70 69-20 Balantrae1237¼ PhantomStorm1181¼ Fillypsser1181 Clipped heels,m rally 8
Claimed from John V Alecci Stable for $12,500, Alecci John V Trainer 2002(as of 07/10): (98 21 14 24 0.21)
25May02-3Pim fst 1 1/16 :233 :48 1:142 1:474 Ⓕ Md Sp Wt 25k **51** 1 31½ 32½ 32 24½ 39½ Karamanos H A L 122 b 2.90 58-32 FreedomOfPort1127¼ Ters'sAngl1222¼ Fillypssr12210 2wd bid 1/4,weakened 7
25Apr02-8Pim fst 6f :232 :47 :594 1:131 3↑ Ⓕ Md 25000 (25-20) **29** 2 7 52¾ 57½ 411 410¾ Karamanos H A L 115 b 2.30 68-17 OblgtonNorth1157¼ LdyZoomZm1222¾ SstyAnn110¾ Urged off rail, empty 9
12Apr02-9Pim fst 6f :231 :47 1:002 1:14 3↑ Ⓕ Md 25000 (25-20) **51** 8 8 67 54 1½ 21 Karamanos H A L 113 b 12.50 74-18 AmeriPrincess1141 Fillypsser1134¼ *AllApologis*1221 3wd,led 1/8,flattened 11
29Mar02-9Lrl fst 6f :231 :473 1:00 1:124 3↑ Ⓕ Md 12500 (12.5-10.5) **47** 3 6 32 21½ 21½ 21½ Johnston M T L 114 b 4.80 73-23 *Punchum*1221½ Fillypasser1143¾ Oh My Lordie1131¼ Chased, flattened out 9
TRAINER: Dirt(85 .06 $1.62) Sprint(50 .04 $2.26) Claim(75 .03 $0.21)

In July and August, Fillypasser had run sprint figures in the mid-to-upper 40's, even competing at a higher class level. Then she bounced down to a 19, recovered somewhat to a 32, but then threw in a real clinker in her last start. Why? Who knows? Perhaps the very slow break had eliminated her. After all, trying to close from a distant last at five furlongs over the Delaware surface—somewhat speed-favoring that day—is straight uphill all the way. It's pretty much hopeless. Whatever the reason for that bad effort, I asked myself: If you excuse that race—pretend it doesn't exist—wouldn't she have the look of a horse cycling up to a better race? One in the 40's, perhaps? Of course, ignoring such terrible-looking performances is a risky business. But the tote board said otherwise. Fillypasser was 21-1, proof that three well-beaten performances in a row will inflate any horse's price—even in this lowly company.

Still, I didn't have enough nerve (or foolhardiness) to key only on Fillypasser, so I looked again at the other four remaining "contenders."

- Little Wilder was 0 for 16 lifetime, mostly at this claiming level. She had just improved from 24 to 32 to 43, her lifetime best effort, so I was concerned about some sort of bounce.

- Absent Ashlee had improved her figures from 10 to 29 to 45 during the summer, and had since run Beyers of 15 and 25. She could again be cycling up to a figure competitive with this bunch.

- Dat Slavic was a second-time starter taking unusually heavy money on the board, opening at 2-1. Perhaps she was not fully fit for her first race and would run much better today.

- Fennel. A first-time starter who was not taking any money at all. So I eliminated her. After all, I reasoned, if you don't get bet in this group, there's little hope for you.

I decided to box Absent Ashlee, Little Wilder, Dat Slavic, and Fillypasser in exactas and trifectas, along with smaller boxes keying Fillypasser first and second with the other three. A small win bet on Fillypasser completed the play.

Fillypasser looked like a winner every step of the way. She moved wide on the turn, drew off as she pleased, and won by six lengths. But the place and show were completely up for grabs. Nobody wanted any part of it until the unbet firster, Fennel (my final elimination) managed to slip in for second. (Actually, the public was right not to bet Fennel. Who would want to play a debut filly who couldn't run more than a 30?!) Little Wilder did indeed decline after the evident strain of her 43 Beyer, but she still stumbled in for third. Absent Ashlee disappointed. And Dat Slavic, despite being bet, actually ran worse than in her first race. All my exactas and trifectas went down the drain.

The Beyer figures had created another huge opportunity. Unfortunately, there's something else the Beyer Speed Figures can't do: They can't go to the windows and make intelligent bets for you. So the smashing victory of Fillypasser turned out to be just another of those annoying bumps on the long parimutuel road.

But we should end this study on a more winning note.

A 2-year-old maiden race is not where you would normally expect the Beyers to show off best. Young runners can be notoriously volatile, their form full of leaps and dives as they grow accustomed to competition and stress, and as they first encounter adverse circumstances or stretch out to unfamiliar distances. And there are not enough races in their past performances to get much of a handle on any figure pattern, or make a judgment about what might be their peak levels of performance. But there are situations even in these frequently inscrutable races where the Beyer figures can help point out a profitable play.

Maiden races are often just a guessing game, but in the second race at Delaware on August 14 you needed fewer guesses than usual. There was only one first-time starter in this field of eight maiden-claiming colts going six furlongs. He was from a barn with little history of success with such horses, and he was taking no money at all on the board (this was well before the disaster with Fennel). Three other runners were well behind in figures. Mauvais Dude, for example, had run a 38 and a 40 in his two lifetime starts at Philadelphia Park, and, even though he had only lost by a half-length in each of those two races, his Beyers were well behind the main contenders and he had failed to improve much in his second start—usually a negative sign for a young horse.

That left four main contenders:

- Gold Pyrite. Trained by the very sharp Julio Cartagena, he had had only one race at Colonial Downs—a five-furlong turf race. Clearly, he was a wild card. There was just no way you could tell what he would do when switched to the dirt at Delaware.

- Cinnamon Ridge. He ran a Beyer of 45 in this class in his only lifetime start. He could certainly improve second time out, especially on first-time Lasix.
- Legendary Prince. He had two races at Calder, where he earned figures of 41 and 47. Just like Mauvais Dude, he had showed only marginal improvement in his second start—definitely not a plus. But he still had to be used.
- Outright Stormy. In his one race he had chased a pace of $21\frac{3}{5}$ in a maiden-special-weight event before fading to finish sixth, $11\frac{1}{2}$ lengths behind. While that effort did not look like much on paper, it had actually earned him a Beyer of 48—making him the top figure horse in the race, and a superb but increasingly rare example of that endangered species, the "hidden fig."

6 Cinnamon Ridge — Own:Marine Robert J — Black, Yellow Diamonds — $50,000
CASTILLO O O (340 41 40 42 .12) 2002:(554 68 .12)
Ch. c. 2 (Feb)
Sire: Mountain Cat (Storm Cat) $15,000
Dam: Lori Sezme(Sezyou)
Br: Karen Silva (Fla)
Tr: Rogers J Michael(68 13 14 10 .19) 2002:(112 27 .24)
L 119

Life	2	M	1	1	$7,950	54	D.Fst	2	0	1	1	$7,950	54
2002	2	M	1	1	$7,950	54	Wet(330)	0	0	0	0	$0	–
2001	0	M	0	0	$0	–	Turf(200)	0	0	0	0	$0	–
Del	2	0	1	1	$7,950	54	Dst(335)	1	0	1	0	$5,200	54

14Aug02-2Del fst 6f :22^2 :46^1 :57 1:12^3 Md 50000 (50-45) **54** 6 5 1^{hd} 1^{hd} 2½ 25¾ Castillo O O L 119 b 2.90 74-13 OtrghtStrmy1195¾ CnnmnRdg1198¾ LgndrPrnc119¾ Vied inside, no match 8
10Jly02-5Del fst 5f :22^1 :47 1:00 Md 50000 (50-45) **45** 7 2 3^2 3½ 32½ 34¾ Castillo O O 118 b 5.10 81-20 WrHwk1181½ PerfectAndRgl1183¼ CinnmonRidg1181¾ Close up, weakened 8
WORKS: Aug10 Del 4f fst :51 B *20/32* Jly6 Del 4f fst :50^1 B *10/32* Jun25 Del 5f fst 1:02^3 Bg*4/16* Jun17 Del 4f fst :50^2 Bg*7/20* Jun12 Del 4f fst :50^3 B *40/69* Jun5 Del 3f fst :37^4 B *9/19*
TRAINER: 2YO(12 .17 $1.15) Dirt(233 .21 $2.29) Sprint(170 .22 $2.23) MdnClm(27 .22 $1.94)

4 Legendary Prince — Own:Kinsman Stable — Blue, Brown Sash — $50,000
MCCARTHY M J (542 107 107 90 .20) 2002:(704 124 .18)
Dk. b or br c. 2 (Apr)
Sire: Concerto (Chief's Crown) $3,500
Dam: Evening Charmer(Woodman)
Br: Kinsman Farms (Fla)
Tr: Nunley Randy(151 20 25 30 .13) 2002:(234 26 .11)
L 120

Life	3	M	0	1	$4,240	47	D.Fst	2	0	0	1	$3,090	47
2002	3	M	0	1	$4,240	47	Wet(344)	1	0	0	0	$1,150	41
2001	0	M	0	0	$0	–	Turf(266)	0	0	0	0	$0	–
Del	1	0	0	1	$2,860	32	Dst(303)	0	0	0	0	$0	–

14Aug02-2Del fst 6f :22^2 :46^1 :57 1:12^3 Md 50000 (50-45) **32** 1 6 72½ 76¼ 4^{10} 314½ Umana J L L 119 b 4.40 65-13 OutrightStormy1195¾ CinnmonRidge1198¾ LegendryPrinc119¾ Gained 3rd 8
Previously trained by Tortora Emanuel
13Jly02-13Crc fst 5f :22^1 :46^4 1:00 Md Sp Wt 23k **47** 1 6 6^8 6^6 6^8 67½ Velasquez C L 118 b 3.30 81-07 *Super Frolic*1182¼ RoyaltyProspect118½ DeputyHalo118¾ Ducked in start 8
22Jun02-10Crc sly 4½f :22^2 :45^4 :52 Md Sp Wt 28k **41** 6 7 58½ 48½ 413½ Velasquez C L 118 *1.60 85-11 Massive118^{12} American Boy1181¼ Tourmendous118^{nk} Failed to menace 8
WORKS: Aug6 Del 5f fst 1:02 B *2/6* Jly27 Del 4f fst :49^3 B *10/30* Jly10 Crc 3f sly :37 Bg(d)*3/12* Jun16 Crc 4f gd :49^4 B *6/15*
TRAINER: 2YO(91 .13 $2.06) Sprint/Route(58 .16 $2.26) Dirt(447 .12 $1.41) MdnClm(129 .13 $1.38)

1 Outright Stormy — Own:Ross Alfred S — Turquoise, Pink Dots
POTTS C L (473 83 65 52 .18) 2002:(491 85 .17)
Dk. b or br c. 2 (Apr) EASMAY02 $26,000
Sire: Storm Creek (Storm Cat) $15,000
Dam: Own It Outright(Rahy)
Br: Farnsworth Farms & Jack T Hammer (Fla)
Tr: Cataldi Tony(83 13 9 9 .16) 2002:(141 22 .16)
115

Life	2	1	0	0	$15,900	68	D.Fst	2	1	0	0	$15,900	68
2002	2	1	0	0	$15,900	68	Wet(335*)	0	0	0	0	$0	–
2001	0	M	0	0	$0	–	Turf(355)	0	0	0	0	$0	–
Del	2	1	0	0	$15,900	68	Dst(325)	0	0	0	0	$0	–

14Aug02-2Del fst 6f :22^2 :46^1 :57 1:12^3 Md 50000 (50-45) **68** 7 1 2^{hd} 2^{hd} 1½ 15¾ Potts C L 119 6.10 80-13 OtrghtStormy1195¾ CnnmnRdg1198¾ LgndryPrnc119¾ 2 wide, steady drive 8
29Jly02-9Del fst 5½f :21^3 :45^3 :58 1:04^3 Md Sp Wt 39k **48** 3 5 52¼ 76¼ 54½ 611½ Black A S 118 31.70 83-14 *CrftyGuy*1185½ ***Legueofhisown***1183¾ Imrelfncydeher118^1 Mild gain inside 10
WORKS: Sep9 Del 5f fst 1:04^3 B *17/18* Sep4 Del 4f fst :50^4 B *[illegible]/76* Aug28 Del 3f fst :39^1 B *28/33* Jly24 Del 4f fst :48^2 B *6/60* Jly17 Del 5f fst 1:02^2 B *10/32* Jly9 Del 5f fst 1:02^1 Bg*5/17*
TRAINER: 2YO(24 .21 $1.83) Sprint/Route(30 .17 $1.82) 31-60Days(46 .24 $2.78) Dirt(224 .17 $1.89) Alw(55 .16 $1.27)

Of course, as we've said before, being the top figure by only one point is virtually meaningless. But the point here is not that Outright Stormy had the top Beyer. Rather, the point is that, against much tougher horses, and chasing a much hotter pace, he had earned a very competitive figure. And today he was dropping from maiden special weight into a $50,000 maiden claimer—a traditionally powerful old handicapping angle that has worked well for decades. The final clincher: He was great value at odds of 6-1.

Strange as it may sound, this obscure example highlights the situations in which the Beyers perform best. Outright Stormy's speed figure did not stand in isolation. It was not his sole recommendation. On the contrary, many other key elements and supporting angles reinforced his solid Beyer:

▸ The classic drop from maiden special weight
▸ The strong pace in his last race
▸ The recency of his form
▸ The value in his price
▸ The relative weakness of his opposition

All these variables added weight to his strong Beyer figure. As with any other single handicapping angle, the Beyers are at their most effective when there is confirmation and support from other evidence and approaches—and when the value is there to make it all worthwhile.

Outright Stormy chased the pace in this race, challenged for the lead on the turn, and then easily drew out to an impressive win.

The case of the unassuming Outright Stormy stresses the value of interrelationships between a variety of handicapping principles. And it demonstrates how the speed figures are strongest when they are primus inter pares. First among equals.